$4.00

COLLECTING

CLOCKS

COLLECTING

CLOCKS

DEREK
ROBERTS

JG
PRESS

A QUANTUM BOOK

Published in the USA 1997 by JG Press.
Distributed by World Publications Inc.

The JG Press imprint is a trademark of
JG Press Inc.
455 Somerset Avenue
North Dighton, MA 02764

This edition produced for sale in the USA, its
territories and dependencies only.

ISBN 1-57215-245-1

QUMCGC

This book was produced by
Quantum Books Ltd
6 Blundell Street
London N7 9BH

Creative Director: Richard Dewing
Designer: Chris Dymond
Project Editor: Judith Simons
Editor: Patricia Bayer

Typeset in Great Britain by
Central Southern Typesetters, Eastbourne
Manufactured in Hong Kong by
Regent Publishing Services Limited
Printed in China by
Leefung-Asco Printers Limited

Contents

Preface and Acknowledgements

This book has been written with the main objectives of showing readers what a fascinating subject horology can be and the enormous range of clocks that have been produced and are available today.

Clocks have the advantage over virtually all other antiques in that they are not only attractive to look at and often fine pieces of furniture, but they are also functional instruments. The early clockmakers were at the forefront of technology and frequently worked with the leading scientists of their day.

It was in clockmaking, too, that the first mass production took place. The concept of freely interchangeable parts led to enormously increased outputs and a corresponding increase in the standard of living, particularly in the United States. The document that brought this about was the famous 'Porter Contract', wherein Eli Terry of Connecticut agreed to supply some 4,000 clocks in three years.

Most of the clocks illustrated in this book are ones that have passed through our hands over the past 20 to 25 years. However, inevitably there were gaps in our photographic library, and we are particularly grateful to all who have helped fill them. The Henry Ford Museum, Dearborn, Michigan, and the National Association of Watch and Clock Collectors, Columbia, Pennsylvania, supplied pictures of American clocks. The Time Museum, Rockford, Illinois, sent pictures of the Gambrinus Chariot Clock, a Hague clock and Black Forest wall clocks. Charles Kengen, Amsterdam, sent pictures of Dutch clocks, and the Science Museum, London, supplied several illustrations.

Others who kindly lent photographs were Sotheby's and Christie's, London; Fanelli Antique Timepieces Ltd, New York, and Keith Banham, London. David Penney supplied the drawings of the verge and anchor escapements and John Martin that of the wagon spring clock. Finally, I should like to acknowledge the great debt I owe to James T West for putting his vast knowledge of American clocks so freely at my disposal. Also, without the enthusiastic help of Julia McCabe, the production of the manuscript for this book would not have been possible. I am extremely grateful to her for all the support she has given me right through from the book's conception to its completion.

Introduction

From their earliest days humans, like most of the animal kingdom, have been aware of time and have been able to estimate it quite accurately, although undoubtedly our ability in this direction has gradually declined with the growth of civilization. It is interesting to note that certain types of insect will repeat particular actions with a variation of no more than a few seconds each day.

As humans gradually progressed, it became necessary to denote time, in order, for instance, to be able to arrange meetings. Probably the first method used on a daily basis was noting the position of a shadow, for instance, that of a tree or a mountain. However, this obviously had its limitations and as man started to live more and more in communities, shadow clocks were erected within them, such as Cleopatra's Needle, the time being marked out on the village square. The next development probably was the small, portable wooden shadow clock, consisting of a horizontal bar with a raised crosspiece on one end, whose shadow would progress along the horizontal bar as the sun rose in the heavens. It had to face east in the morning and west in the afternoon. The final and most popular development of this method of timekeeping was the garden sundial.

Obviously, all these methods of determining time were fine in sunny areas such as the Middle East, one of the cradles of ancient civilization, but they would be far less practical in many other areas and of no use at all at night. To overcome this problem, various other forms of timekeepers were devised, such as the sandglass, in which time is measured by the running of sand through a narrow orifice from one container to another. Water clocks (clepsydras) based on a similar principle were also devised, and fire clocks, too, came into common use. Probably the simplest of these was a candle graduated down its length in hours. Other types of timekeeper were based on the reduction of the level of oil in a lamp or the slow burning of powder along a grooved channel.

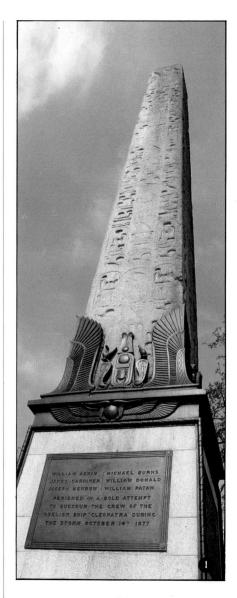

— **1** —

CLEOPATRA'S NEEDLE

This obelisk was built at Heliopolis in Egypt by the Pharaoh Thothmes III about 1500 BC. Although a decorative and symbolic structure, in effect it would have been one of several giant sundials predating our public clocks by nearly 3,000 years. It was brought to England in 1877 and now stands on the Thames Embankment, London. Another Cleopatra's Needle stands in Central Park in New York City, where it was moved from Heliopolis in 1880.

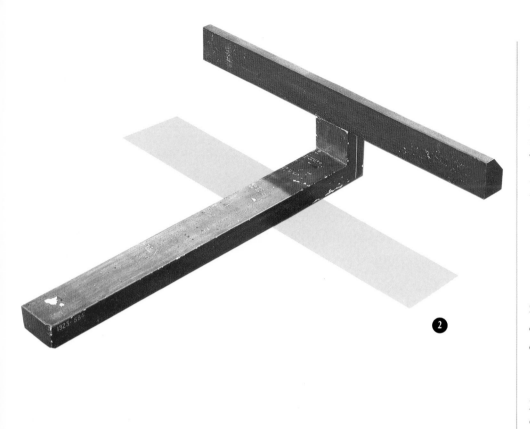

2

PORTABLE SHADOW CLOCK

A copy of an early (*c*8th–10th century BC) shadow clock. It was placed due east in the morning and west in the afternoon. The time was indicated by the shadow from the crossbar falling on the base, on which the hours were inscribed.

— **3** —

SET OF FOUR SANDGLASSES, PROBABLY ITALIAN, C1720

Studs on the ebony and ivory frame indicate how long each sandglass takes to empty: one stud, ¼ hour; two studs, ½ hour; three studs, ¾ hour; 4 studs, 1 hour. Each of the four sandglasses is joined at the centre and filled with fine emery powder.

3

The Mechanical Clock
· · · · · ·

The birth of the mechanical clock, as it is known today, probably took place at the end of the 13th or the beginning of the 14th century. This was made possible by the invention of the verge and foliot escapement, which works on the principle of a vertical arbor (axle) on which a horizontally oscillating bar is mounted. Flags attached to the arbor alternately stop and release the teeth of a wheel (the escape wheel), with which other wheels and pinions engage that are used to indicate time, usually by means of hands attached to them. The Dover Castle Clock is one of the oldest examples that still has its original verge and foliot escapement.

— 4 —

DOVER CASTLE CLOCK, C1600

This is one of the oldest clocks that still has its original verge escapement with foliot from which the regulating weights may be seen hanging. The balance oscillates once every eight seconds, and the gearing is such that this allows the great wheel to rotate once every hour.

The going train may be seen in the foreground with its large wooden barrel with capstan for winding it. In the centre of the clock is the countwheel controlling the strike and behind it is the strike train. Note the simple construction of the frame held together with iron pegs, more reminiscent of the work of a blacksmith than that of a clockmaker.

This clock was transferred from Dover Castle, Kent, to the Science Museum, London, in 1872.

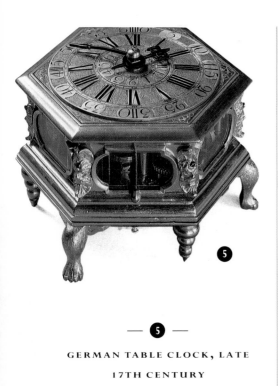

— ❺ —

**GERMAN TABLE CLOCK, LATE
17TH CENTURY**

Clocks of this type were produced from
the late 16th century until well into the
18th century. The cases were of fire-gilt
brass, usually either round or four-, six-
or eight-sided. They were of short duration and often of considerable complexity,
sometimes featuring an alarm and quite
frequently being quarter-striking.

The clock seen here, some 6 in
(15 cm) across, has grande-sonnerie
striking and an alarm.

It is likely that many of the early clocks had no dial or hands but
merely struck the hours, frequently to call people to prayers (nearly all
these clocks were made for ecclesiastical use). The earliest mechanical
clocks still in existence in England are those of Exeter, Salisbury and
Wells cathedrals.

Whereas domestic clocks did not come into use in England until
around 1600, they appeared far earlier on the Continent and in particular in southern Germany, around Augsburg and Nuremberg. The
oldest examples were weight-driven wall clocks, almost always of
short duration, but the invention of the coiled spring around AD 1500
enabled a whole range of spring-driven table clocks to be produced;
these were much more portable than weight-driven clocks and were
often of considerable complexity. The coiled spring also directly resulted in the birth of the watch, which it made possible.

The early watches and small spring clocks employing a balance
were relatively inaccurate. It was only around the year 1670 when the
hairspring, used to control the balance, was invented that the perfor-
mance of such timepieces dramatically improved.

On most early turret clocks the foliot controlled timekeeping, with
weights being moved, added to or removed from the bar to slow or
speed it. However, on later domestic clocks, particularly the English
lantern clock that started to be produced around 1600, a large balance
wheel was usually preferred.

The Pendulum

A dramatic improvement in timekeeping took place in the mid 17th
century as a result of the discovery of the pendulum. This followed on
Leonardo da Vinci's famous observation in a cathedral that no matter
how wide the arc of swing of a chandelier, the time it took to move
from one side to the other was always the same. However, it was left
to Christiaan Huygens, the Dutch mathematician, and Salomon Coster,
an eminent Dutch clockmaker, to apply the principle of the pendulum
to a clock, which they did in 1657. In a very short time this idea spread
throughout Europe and in particular to England. Early pendulum
clocks used a verge escapement.

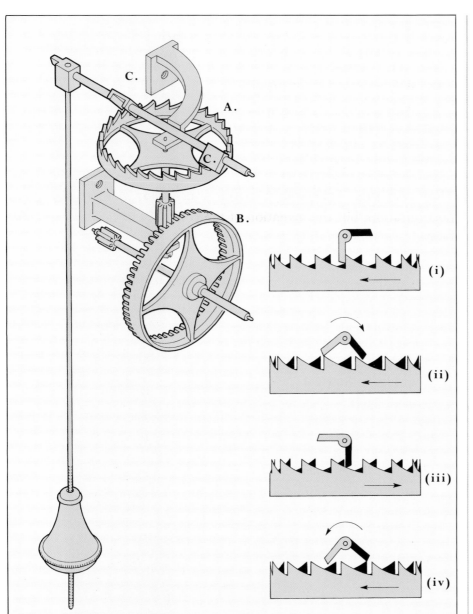

The Verge Escapement

1   When the pendulum is at the extreme right of its swing, the front of the two verge pallets is engaged with vertical face of a 'scape wheel tooth. The tooth gives impulse to the pendulum through the pallet.

2   As the pendulum swings from right to left, the front pallet unlocks from the 'scape wheel.

3   The rear verge pallet now engages a tooth on the other side of the 'scape wheel; the momentum of the pendulum causes the 'scape wheel to recoil until the pendulum comes to rest at the left of its swing.

4   The sequence of events is then repeated, but with the pendulum swinging from left to right.

— ❻ —

GAMBRINUS CHARIOT
CLOCK, C1600

Many complex clocks, often incorporating automata (moving parts), were made in Augsburg in southern Germany during the 16th and 17th centuries. This particularly fine example depicts the gluttonous mythical King Gambrinus, who is associated with brewing beer. The clock was designed so that either at the hour or when activated it proceeds down a banqueting table; as it does so the king raises and lowers his right hand containing the beer mug and at the same time opens and closes his mouth.

Longcase Clocks

T he invention of the pendulum in the mid 17th century gave rise to the longcase, primarily as a box to protect it and conceal the relatively unsightly weights, pulleys and lines or ropes.

The pendulums used in conjunction with the verge escapement were short, averaging maybe 9 in (23 cm) in length and having a wide arc of swing. Because the pendulum was short it could be accommodated within a narrow case, usually only around 6 ft 3 in (1.9 m) high, which, in keeping with the Puritan influence then prevailing, was black, either making use of ebony veneers or ebonized fruitwood.

The Anchor Escapement and the 'Royal' Pendulum

To have had a longer pendulum would have made it impossible to confine it within the case and, moreover, would have absorbed far more power. However, around 1670 the anchor escapement was invented, most likely by William Clement. The basic difference between this and the verge, which was used virtually universally up until that time, is that the escape wheel is mounted parallel to all the other wheels in the clock and thus no contrate wheel is needed. It also requires a far narrower arc of swing and thus a much longer pendulum can be accommodated within a narrow case. This immediately made possible what became known as the 'royal' pendulum, approximately 3.28 ft (1 metre) in length, which moved from side to side (beat) in exactly one second.

The principal advantages of these new developments were twofold: the accuracy of clocks increased dramatically, and seconds could now be shown by a separate hand on the dial directly connected to the arbor (axle) on which the pallets are mounted.

— ❶ —

ENGLISH LONGCASE CLOCK,
PROBABLY BY THE
FROMANTEELS, C1670—75

The earliest longcase clocks were small (usually less than 6½ ft/1.98 m tall) and ebony-veneered. Their simple classical proportions, based on Roman and Greek architecture, have seldom been equalled, let alone improved upon.

This fine example, almost certainly by the Fromanteels, has panelled sides and a three-panelled door hung directly in the unframed trunk. The backboard extends up above the rising hood, which is provided with a spoon lock and catch. The hood has wooden columns which possess fine gilt brass capitols

The latched six-pillar movement has circular cutouts at the top of the plates, as favoured by some early makers, and rests on blocks. It has a verge escapement with bob pendulum and external countwheel strike with a vertically pivoted hammer.

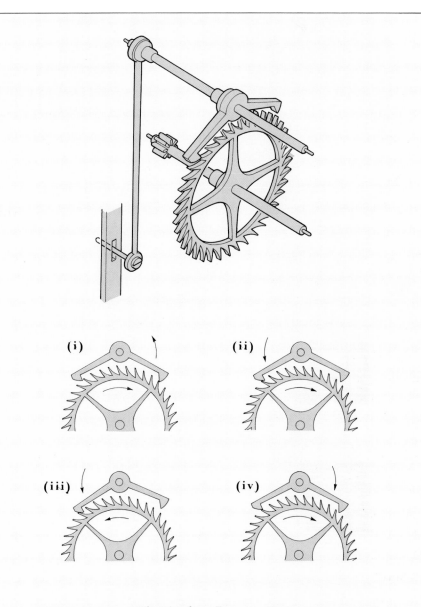

The Anchor Escapement

The anchor escapement is simpler than the verge escapement; no contrate wheel is required because the 'scape wheel is in the same plane as the other wheels in the train. A further difference is that the pallets are not directly connected to the pendulum.

1   The pendulum of the clock is swinging to the right and the 'scape wheel is about to be released by the right-hand (exit) pallet.

2   As the pendulum continues its swing, the wheel is released, but is almost immediately arrested again by the left-hand (entry) pallet.

3   This causes the wheel to recoil.

4   As the pendulum swings back to the left, the 'scape wheel is released by the left hand-pallet; and the right-hand pallet (and thus the pendulum) receives an impulse after it has contacted the 'scape wheel.

ENGLISH LONGCASE CLOCK, EDWARD EAST, LONDON, C1680

This early (*c*1680) walnut longcase clock by the eminent maker, Edward East, is seen here just as it was discovered some 15 to 20 years ago. Note the delicate cherub spandrels, the narrow chapter, the relatively large but thin seconds rings, both of which would originally have been silvered, and the fine steel hands. The walnut case, a little distressed where it has been kicked on its base over the years, is of excellent proportions, with a long narrow door going almost out to the edge of the trunk. Its walnut veneers are anything up to ⅛ in (3 mm) thick.

ENGLISH LONGCASE CLOCK, WILLIAM SPEAKMAN, LONDON, C1685

The first decoration to appear on the early walnut and olivewood veneered longcases was parquetry, of which this clock by William Speakman is a particularly good example. Speakman, a very early London clockmaker, was apprenticed to Nicholas Tomlins on 25 August 1654 and subsequently turned over to Peter Closon or Andrew Prime. He gained his Freedom of the Worshipful Clockmakers Company in 1661 and rose to become Master in 1701.

The lift-up hood has spiral twist columns, glazed sides and an attractive cushion mould beneath the flat top. Below the hood is a relatively shallow convex mould. The sides of the trunk are panelled and crossbanded with boxwood and ebony stringing surrounding olivewood oysters. The whole of the front of the case is also decorated with fine olivewood oysters and olivewood crossbanding, with a strip of

boxwood crossbanding and ebony string-ing on the inner aspect of the door and around the lenticle. The base rests on bun feet.

Various parquetry designs decorate the front of the case. There is a fan inlay at the four corners of the base and a circle in the centre. The trunk door has semicircles at the top and bottom and full circles of parquetry above and below the lenticle with two small circles with eight-pointed star parquetry above and below the upper circle.

The good five-pillar movement has the countwheel mounted behind the great wheel and, interestingly, it has an alarm. There are brass cased weights.

The 10 in (25.4 cm) square dial has the largest form of cherub spandrels, a narrow seconds ring with a cutout for the central alarm disc and a date aperture immediately above 6 o'clock. The ends of the winding squares are crossed and the holes are plain, ie, not ringed. There are delicate half-hour marks.

This is a most attractive clock of small size, good proportions and excellent col-our, and it is decorated with fine veneers.

Height: 6 ft 5 in (1.96 m).

Maintaining Power
· · · · · ·

Following Clement's invention there were no major advances in the design of the mechanical components of a longcase clock for the next 250 years. However, one improvement introduced into the construction of the longcase clock in the 1670s was 'maintaining power'. With this an auxiliary spring is brought into play that keeps the clock going while it is being wound and power is removed from the train of wheels. The first form was known as 'bolt and shutter', wherein shutters covered the winding holes and could only be removed by pulling a cord or depressing a lever. This action also charged a spring-loaded bolt, which pressed on one of the wheels in the clock and kept it going.

This form of maintaining power gave considerable trouble and its use largely had been discontinued by 1700. For the same reason it has usually been removed from earlier clocks and where it is seen, it is generally a reinstatement. A more efficient method of maintaining power, known as 'Harrison's going ratchet', was devised in the 1720s.

The Dial
· · · · · ·

The earliest longcase clocks were small, usually no more than 6 ft 4 in (1.9 m), but as the 17th century progressed they gradually got taller, probably averaging 7 ft (2.1 m) without a caddy and 7 ft 5 in (2.26 m) with one by around 1700. At the same time the dials, always square, got larger, being 10 in (25.4 cm) or less in the early days, then 11 in (28 cm) and finally 12 in (30.5 cm), a size that was to stay by far the most popular for the rest of the life of the longcase clock.

A major change occurred around 1710–15, when an arch was added to the top of the square dial. This gave additional space on which to place various features such as a name plaque, strike/silent regulation or calendar work. Although at least 95 per cent of the clocks made in London after this time employed the breakarch, the square dial never went entirely out of fashion, particularly in the country, and it continued to be used well into the 19th century.

Case Styles

In London walnut was the most popular wood for veneering clock cases once ebony had gone out of fashion, whereas in the country from the earliest times oak had been popular. Sometimes the walnut was highly figured and in other cases relatively plain.

MARQUETRY

By the 1670s, as the austere influence of the Puritans declined, ebonized cases started to give way to cases veneered in woods such as walnut and olivewood. It was not long before these were decorated, first with parquetry, which is formed from geometric designs let into the case, and subsequently marquetry, usually floral and often with birds.

At first marquetry was confined to panels laid on the trunk door and base, but subsequently it spread to involve the hood and gradually most of the case. Toward the end of the 17th century floral marquetry started to give way to arabesques, which comprise bold contrasting strapwork, usually in a dark wood laid on a light background and frequently incorporating figures, butterflies and birds. The final development of marquetry is known as 'seaweed', which consists of a delicate tracery usually employing only two different woods.

Although marquetry developed roughly in the order described above, there was overlap of styles. Also, it was by no means unusual to see floral marquetry in use as late as 1710, and it even staged a brief revival in the Victorian and Edwardian eras. However, at roughly the same time as the breakarch style came into favour, the use of marquetry became unfashionable.

CHINOISERIE OR LACQUER WORK

This is the decoration of furniture and other objects with gilded gesso (a form of plasterwork), which is laid on a japanned or hard coloured lacquered background. Its use in the Far East goes back at least 2,000 years, but it only appeared in Europe following increased trade with the Orient in the 15th century, first from Venice and Genoa, then Portugal and, finally, The Netherlands and England some 200 years later. In the early 1600s probably only small pieces such as tea caddies were imported, but later larger items such as wall panels were shipped back. However, it was very rare for large pieces of furniture to be imported and the number of pieces sent out to the Far East for decoration was very small.

— ❹ —

ENGLISH FLORAL MARQUETRY LONGCASE CLOCK, 1695

Floral marquetry followed hard on the heels of parquetry. At first its use was confined to the trunk and base of the clock and it was only employed in panels, but it rapidly spread to involve the hood and eventually was laid all over the clock, ie, not just in the panels. Note the beautiful array of flowers incorporated in the example seen here. The earliest marquetry tended to be quite bold in concept, whereas later examples were more detailed.

— **5** —

ENGLISH MARQUETRY LONGCASE CLOCK, ROBERT DINGLEY, LONDON, C1685

Seen here is a beautifully proportioned little marquetry longcase clock with a trunk only 10½ in (26.6 cm) wide. The door is decorated with panels of floral marquetry, the central one inhabited by a bird. The rest of the surface has olive-wood oyster veneers, and it has a brass-ringed lenticle. Surrounding the panels is boxwood stringing and around the edge of the door is an ebony mould beyond which is olivewood crossbanding. The sides of the case are decorated with olive-wood oysters and have boxwood cross-banding. The sides of the forward-sliding hood are glazed and there are applied turned columns on its door. The base is panelled and cross-banded and rests on bun feet.

The fine month-duration movement has five latched pillars and employs an external countwheel. An unusual feature, which occurs occasionally during this period, is a striking train that has been placed on the right instead of in the standard position on the left. The 10 in (25.4 cm) square brass dial has well-executed cherub spandrels, a raised chapter ring with delicate half-hour marks, seconds below 12 o'clock, a date aperture immediately above 6 o'clock and a well-matted centre.

The clock is signed along the bottom edge 'Robert Dingley, London', a fine maker who was apprenticed to Lionel Wyth on 1 July 1661, became a Freeman of The Clockmakers Company in 1668 and remained a member of the company until 1706. His work is similar to that of Joseph Knibb.

Height: 6 ft 3½ in (1.92 m).

5

— **6** —

ENGLISH LONGCASE CLOCK, DANIEL DELANDER, LONDON, C1715

This clock is an example of the high-quality pieces that were being produced in the first part of the 18th century, when the leading English clockmakers were vying with each other to make the finest and most complex clocks, sometimes of long duration, maybe quarter-chiming or musical, and occasionally incorporating astronomical features.

The Movement and Dial The month-duration movement of this clock is of excellent quality, having five latched pillars and bolt-and-shutter maintaining power. The 13 in (33 cm) square brass dial has a very shallow arch on it in which are displayed three rings that are, from the outside in: Year Calendar; Equation of Time, that is the difference between the sun's (solar) time and our (mean) time; and Sun, Slow/Fast. Beneath this is the inscription 'The Equation of Natural Days'. On either side of this are highly unusual spandrels depicting heraldic birds. The four urn corner spandrels are also of fine quality and individual design. The chapter ring has quartering on its inner aspect; half-hour diamonds and half-quarter marks on the outer edge.

The clock is signed by Daniel Delander and is indeed typical of his work. Delander was an extremely fine and ingenious maker famed for his equation work and his duplex escapement. Examples of his work are in numerous collections and museums (a year-duration equation clock was in the famous Wetherfield Collection, which was sold and dispersed in 1928). He started work in 1692, gained his Freedom of The Clockmakers Company in 1699 and died in 1733.

The Case The case of this clock is of the

finest quality, with carefully chosen and beautifully figured burr walnut veneers laid on an oak carcass. Its proportions, too, are excellent. All the moulds are cross grain. There is a caddy top sur-mounted by three finials and featuring a fret below. The hood door has applied brass-capped pillars and seems to have its original glazing. There is glass on either side of the hood and frets are found immediately above.

The sides of the trunk and base are panelled. There is a double plinth and a rectangular trunk door. This and the rudimentary breakarch would suggest a date of manufacture of *c*1715.

Height to top of finial: 9 ft 4 in (2.8 m).

— **7** —

ENGLISH LACQUER LONGCASE CLOCK, HENRY FISH, LONDON, C1720

Although lacquer clocks had begun to be made in England at the end of the 17th century, it was not until around 1720 that they were being produced in any numbers. Earlier decoration, such as on this clock, is relatively bold.

The dark lacquer case, which has applied brass-capped pillars and glazing on the sides of the hood, is attractively decorated with gilt gesso work depicting flowers, foliage, people, a building beside a lake and different kinds of birds. An interesting feature of this clock is that the raised work is not just confined to the trunk door.

The good five-pillar movement has rack strike and a 12 in (30.5 cm) square brass dial with a raised chapter ring which has half-hour marks, quartering on its inner edge, a seconds ring, date aperture with engraving around, ringed winding holes and twin cherub and crown spandrels.

Height: 7 ft (2.13 m).

Lacquer decoration first started to be used on furniture in The Netherlands *c*1660 and somewhat later than this in England. However, it was probably never used on clock cases prior to 1690. Considerable numbers of lacquer clocks were produced in the period 1710–30, but lacquering never completely went out of fashion and in fact it staged a quite strong recovery under the influence of such leading cabinetmakers as Chippendale in the third quarter of the 18th century.

Black was probably the most common colour used, but various forms of red, tortoiseshell and green were also employed. White is rarely seen on these clocks.

MAHOGANY

The decline in popularity of walnut furniture that started in the 1720s was due to a combination of factors, one of these being the decreasing supply, largely due to the loss through disease of many walnut trees, particularly in France. Indeed, the situation became so serious in that country that its export was banned. Another strong influence was the increasing import of mahogany from the West Indies and America following England's rapidly growing trade in those areas. The timber that the English imported, mainly from Cuba and Honduras, was ideal for cabinetmaking: it was not subject to attack by worm (as was walnut), it was available in long, wide boards and it could also be obtained highly figured, such natural patterning being ideal for veneers.

The earlier mahogany clock cases tended not to be highly figured, but by 1765–85 cases of the very highest quality with superb veneers were being produced. However, by the end of the century only a small number of longcase clocks were still being produced in London, and those made in the Regency period tended to have circular dials, either painted or of silvered brass.

8

— 8 —

The classic London mahogany pagoda-topped longcase clock gradually evolved over a period of some 40 to 50 years. It was developed from and succeeded the caddy top, the earliest examples being seen on walnut and lacquer cases. By the middle of the 18th century mahogany was being used extensively. At first the timber was fairly plain and sometimes employed in the solid, but by the 1770s beautifully figured veneers were being applied to the case.

At the same time brass stringing was added to the hood columns and brass-capped quarter columns were frequently applied to either side of the trunk. The wooden fret employed in the pagoda to let the sound out was sometimes replaced by a decorative brass fret. The clock cases produced in London at that time were among the finest ever made.

In this example the quality features mentioned above can be seen, plus other details such as a shaped panelled base, a well-executed mould around the trunk door and a classic 'London' 12 in (30.5 cm) dial, with finely matted centre and strike/silent regulation in the arch.

COUNTRY MAHOGANY LONGCASE CLOCKS

Whereas clocks produced in London tended to be standardized in design, those made outside the capital showed far more individuality and frequently developed regional characteristics. For instance, in the West Country, as befits a seafaring area, the clocks frequently featured rolling moon discs in the arch with ships and often showed the time of high water at a particular port. A wavy border was sometimes a part of the inner aspect of the hood door and rope-twist columns were also popular decorative devices.

When the town where the clock was made was close to the capital, then the influence of London designs was strong, with similar designs used in a somewhat simplified form. However, in more remote areas entirely different designs evolved: for instance, the swan-neck pediment, immensely popular in the country, was scarcely ever seen on London-made clocks.

Thirty-Hour Clocks
· · · · · · ·

The term '30 hour' really implies a clock that will run a little more than a day, so that if you wind it a few hours later than usual it does not stop. Very few were made in London but they were particularly popular in the country districts because of their small size and relatively affordable cost.

Up until around 1770 they usually had solid oak cases and a square brass dial, frequently 10 in (25.4 cm), but on the later clocks 11 in (28 cm) or 12 in (30.5 cm) square. The early clocks only had a single hand, ie, no minutes were indicated, and virtually all 30-hour clocks are driven by a single weight that is rewound every day by pulling down on a rope or chain. An advantage of this is that maintaining power is provided, ie, the clock is kept going while being wound, and also no winding holes are required in the dial.

Toward the end of the 18th century mahogany cases were employed far more frequently, usually in conjunction with a painted dial. By then, however, their production was seriously waning relative to the eight-day clock.

9

— **9** —

ENGLISH LONGCASE CLOCK,

JEREMIAH STANDRING,

BOLTON, C1780

Whereas the longcase clocks produced in London tended to be standardized, those made in the provinces varied far more greatly, particularly from region to region. Some would even say that clocks from the provinces had far more character. Their quality, especially in the last half of the 18th century, was often excellent.

A typical example is this Lancashire clock. It is surmounted by a swan neck, a feature virtually never seen on London clocks, and there is no brass stringing on the hood or quarter columns of the trunk. However, the proportions are good and the standard of manufacture is excellent. In fact, the cases were often made by eminent cabinetmakers, such as Gillows of Lancaster.

A particularly attractive feature of this longcase clock is its dial, with a beautifully engraved centre, large cherub spandrels and the phases of the moon shown in the arch of the dial.

Height: 7 ft 10 in (2.39 m)

— ⑩ —

**ENGLISH 30-HOUR OAK
LONGCASE CLOCK,
GEORGE DONISTHORPE,
BIRMINGHAM, C1780**

From the early 1700s onward, simple longcase clocks of only 30-hour duration started to be made for farmworkers' cottages. These were usually less than 6½ ft (1.98 m) tall to suit the low ceilings and the earlier clocks generally had a 10 in (24.5 cm) square brass dial with just a single (hour) hand that was quite accurate enough for the owners' lifestyles.

As the century progressed the addition of the minute hand became common, and the dial became somewhat larger, either 11 in (28 cm) or 12 in (30.5 cm), as seen on the clock shown here.

By 1780–90 the painted dial had largely replaced the brass dial and more decorative cases, often veneered in mahogany, were produced. However, by then the manufacture of 30-hour clocks was rapidly declining in favour of those that had an eight-day duration.

⑩

The White- or Painted-Dial Longcase Clock

· · · · · ·

Very few painted-dial longcase clocks were made in London, but from 1780 they achieved great popularity elsewhere. Before the century was out they were probably outselling brass-dial clocks ten to one.

The first recorded reference to white dials, unearthed by Brian Loomes, appeared in the *Birmingham Gazette* in 1772. It read as follows:

Osborne and Wilson, manufacturers of white clock dials in imitation of enamel, in a manner entirely new, have opened a warehouse at No 3 in Colmore Row, Birmingham. Where they have an assortment of the above mentioned goods. Those who favour them with orders may depend upon their being executed with the utmost punctuality and expedition.

The earliest white dials sometimes had no decoration other than the numerals and the signature, or just spandrels in the form of raised gilt decoration in the four corners. However, they rapidly became more colourful, typically displaying flowers such as roses and peonies in the corners and, if there was no moon disc, also in the arch. If there was a moon disc and the clock was made near the coast, particularly in the West Country, then ships were featured, but inland buildings were often chosen, at least in part, as the subject. A popular feature was to illustrate the four seasons by means of flowers, crops or girls dressed in suitable costumes or carrying out activities associated with the different times of the year.

As the 19th century progressed, the decoration on the dial increased, the corners being filled in solid and scenes and people depicted in the arch. Indeed, by the 1850s, shortly before the demise of the longcase clock, virtually the whole of the dial was covered with decoration.

Complex Clocks

· · · · · ·

A considerable number of complex clocks were made, mostly in the period 1720–80. Some of these would chime the quarters, usually on eight bells, and others would play a tune either every one or three hours or at will. Others gave complex astronomical information.

A further complexity sometimes added to a clock's design was to make it go for longer than one week. A month was the period most often chosen and this was particularly popular from 1670 to 1710, but clocks of three, six and even 12 months running were also made.

— 11 —

ENGLISH WHITE-PAINTED DIAL
LONGCASE CLOCK,
JOHN CHAPMAN,
LOUGHBOROUGH, C1790

The white-painted dial longcase clock started to appear in the 1770s and rapidly replaced the brass dial outside London. They had the advantage, in that they were easier to read, cheaper to produce and many would say far more decorative, such as the example by Chapman seen here. Each of the girls in the four corners is appropriately dressed for performing activities representing the four seasons. Note the display of moon phases in the arch incorporating a ship, a favourite feature, and the use of brass hands (which would not be employed on a brass dial, as they would be difficult to see).

The case, with swan-neck pediment, is of fine quality with a beautifully figured door and base panel surmounted by cross-banding. There are brass-capped quarter columns on either side of the trunk.

Height: 7 ft 4 in (2.24 m).

⓬

ENGLISH QUARTER-CHIMING AND TIDAL-DIAL LONGCASE CLOCK WITH YEAR CALENDAR, CHARLES CLAY, LONDON, C1725

This fine-quality longcase clock is by Charles Clay, who is justly famous for his musical, in particular organ, clocks.

The case is a good example of the fully developed breakarch top, with substantial cross-grain moulds and a sound fret below; freestanding pillars on the hood and frets on either side. The trunk door, which repeats the breakarch of the hood and dial, is surrounded by crossbanding and has cross-grain moulds. The base panel of the clock is quartered and stands on a double plinth.

The spectacular and very carefully laid out dial has a rectangular part 14 in (35.5 cm) high and 13 in (33 cm) wide, the extra height permitting much larger subsidiary dials than would normally be the case. At the top left of the dial is regulation for silent quarters, strike all and silent all, much in the style used by some of the finer makers in the 17th century, and at the top right the months of the year are shown.

A superb feature of the clock is a silvered ring in the arch, some 7¼ in (18.4 cm) in diameter, which shows the age of the moon and the time of high water, presumably at London Bridge. In the centre is a star-studded disc that revolves, and as it does so it displays the various phases of the moon.

A rear view of the seven pillar movement would show eight bells for the chime with the hour bell, partially covering them, nestling between the winged extensions on either side. The extensions carry the calendar work and the strike/silent regulation.

Height: 8 ft (2.44 m).

— ⓭ —

ENGLISH ASTRONOMICAL LONGCASE CLOCK, EDWARD COCKEY, WARMINSTER, C1710

This is a remarkable example of country clockmaking. It illustrates the superb craftsmanship and artistry of the finest early clockmakers, who set a standard seldom equalled – let alone excelled – as the century progressed.

The clock dates from the first decade of the 18th century and is one of four clocks in existence today that are known to have been made by Edward Cockey of Warminster. It has a movement of three-month duration with recoil escapement and one-and-a-quarter-seconds pendulum. The driving weight housed in the Corinthian column at the front of the case is 90 lb (43 kg) and the clock is wound through the contrate wheel driving onto a wheel mounted on the front of the barrel. Access to the winding square is through the left-hand side of the clock's hood.

The dial plate is 20 in (51 cm) square and carries a 24-hour chapter ring. Within this is set a dish that rotates once every 24 hours. This dish is painted to represent the day and night skies and carries, among other images, a gilt representation of the sun. The dish revolves behind a painted fixed shield that fully obscures the celestial scene between the hours of 8:45 PM and 3:45 AM. Appearing from each side of this shield are blued-steel shutters that rise and fall to ensure that the image of the sun rises and sets at the correct times on each day.

The sunrise/sunset shutters are controlled through arms that ride on large cams, each of which is attached to one of two 9 in (23 cm) diameter wheels with 365 teeth rotating once a year. Fitted to the bottom shield is a 10 in (25.4 cm) diameter brass ring, decorated with wheat-ear engraving, which acts as a guide to the inner edges of the sunrise/

sunset shutters. Within this fixed ring is a blued-steel, wavy-edged ring that rotates with a celestial dish and to which is attached a cast gilt figure of Father Time. His hand indicates the hour, while the minutes are shown by a long gilt centre-sweep hand.

Within the blue wavy ring three concentric silvered rings are set. The outer is a year calendar, the next represents the ecliptic divided into 360 degrees of the zodiac, and within that are shown the 29½ days of one lunation.

The calendar and zodiac scales are fixed together and are read from the pierced gilt pointer fitted to the blue ring at 90 degrees from Father Time. These two rings have been moved 11 days relative to each other during the 18th century to correct for the changeover, in 1752, to the Gregorian Calendar. The age of

the moon, read from the inner of the three rings, is indicated by the right foot of Father Time. Set within the lunar calendar, in a blued plate with gilt stars, is a moon ball that rotates about a radial axis to show its phases. In the centre of the dial, set on a silvered plate engraved to show clouds and rain, is a representation of the earth. It is interesting to note that viewed from the earth, the sun and the moon always maintain their correct relative positions in the zodiac.

The design of the four large spandrels' ornaments is unique to Cockey and is thought to represent the seated figure of Queen Anne.

The clock is housed in a reproduction case that has been carefully copied from that of a similar clock by Cockey to be found in the National Maritime Museum, Greenwich, London.

French Longcase Clocks

Virtually no longcase clocks, in the English sense of the term, were produced in France. However, the French did make clocks that resembled English models in some ways. In the 18th century, for example, the French sometimes placed their clocks on decorative matching pillars, which in effect gave them roughly the height and width of a longcase clock. Also, from 1760 onward they housed their regulators in far more restrained one-piece cases of superb quality, which by 1780–1810 were often free of all ornamentation.

Considerable numbers of what might be termed longcases were made in the country districts of France in the 19th century to house what were known as Comtoise clocks (from the clockmaking district, Franche-Comté). These usually had ornamental, thin-pressed brass dials with enamelled centres and frequently very large and decorative pendulums, although on the earlier clocks these tended to be plain. The cases were usually made of local woods such as apple, cherry or pine. A characteristic feature of these clocks was that they struck at the hour and then repeated it again at two minutes past.

The American Longcase Clock
. . . . . .

The earliest clocks to appear in the New World undoubtedly would have been those brought over by the first settlers. It is probable that these would have been relatively small clocks such as lanterns, not longcase clocks, which would have been expensive to transport. Among these early settlers were an ever increasing number of blacksmiths and clockmakers. Abel Cottey (d 1717) from Crediton in Devon was one of the first recorded craftsmen, having emigrated in 1682 to Philadelphia, where he is known to have prospered and made longcase clocks.

By the early 18th century clockmaking was fairly well established in New York, New England, Pennsylvania and Virginia, and was conducted much as it was back in England at that time. As the 18th century progressed, clockmaking gradually spread over a much wider area, although certain places, such as Connecticut, became important centres for the craft.

The basic methods of clock construction in the American colonies were similar to those used in England, but they had to be adapted to local needs, often because of a lack of suitable materials. Brass, for instance, was in short supply, and to overcome this problem the metal was sometimes used in strip form or wood was used as a substitute. Similarly, local woods such as cherry were employed for the case.

Although some complete longcase clocks were obviously imported, in the majority of instances probably just movements were brought in (complete with dials) and the cases manufactured locally. A great deal of components were also imported, sometimes whole movements and dials, but in other instances just wheels, pinions, barrels, plates, hands, pendulum bobs and so on.

Prior to the War of Independence it is likely that only a fairly small but gradually increasing number of longcase – or tall-case as they are referred to in the United States – clocks were produced. By the early 19th century the first examples of smaller mass-produced clocks were starting to appear. The Willards of Massachusetts evolved their own style of case and movement in the guise of the banjo clock, and Gideon Roberts in Bristol, Connecticut, produced wall clocks with wooden movements. But it is Eli Terry of Connecticut who is credited with making the first mass-produced clocks in 1806, when he filled an order for 4,000 of them.

— **14** —

AMERICAN TALL-CASE CLOCK, AARON WILLARD, BOSTON, MASSACHUSETTS, C1800

The Willards were one of the most important families in the history of American clockmaking, starting with the manufacture of traditional English handcrafted clocks and continuing through into the era of volume production.

Aaron Willard (1757–1844), maker of the clock illustrated here, produced more clocks than his other brothers, but Simon (1753–1848) was the innovator. He made, for instance, the banjo wall clock, which was the first successful, truly American design.

This clock has a mahogany-veneered pine case with an arched hood surmounted by pierced fretwork and three brass finials. The sides of the hood are glazed. The rectangular trunk door has moulded edges and a band of stringing with brass-capped quarter columns on either side.

The brass eight-day, weight-driven movement, with rack strike on a bell, has a white-painted metal dial with Roman hour and Arabic minute numerals, seconds below 12 o'clock, floral decoration on the four corners and a ship rocking to and fro in the arch.

Overall height: 7 ft 10½ in (2.40 m).

— **15** —

TALL CLOCK, ISAAC BROKAW, BRIDGE TOWN, NEW JERSEY, C1810

Isaac Brokaw was apprenticed to Aaron Miller. He completed his apprenticeship and married Miller's daughter in 1766, and continued in business until 1816.

The eight-day movement is typical of his later work, having brass instead of

wood winding-drums and brass instead of steel pillars. An inside countwheel strike is used.

The Federal case, made of and veneered in mahogany, is typical of east New Jersey's finest cabinet makers, such as Oliver Parsell and Matthew Edgerton Jr of New Brunswick.

— 16 —

AMERICAN TALL-CASE CLOCK, THOMAS HARLAND, NORWICH, CONNECTICUT

In 1773 Thomas Harland came from England to Norwich, Connecticut, where he continued to make clocks in the traditional English way. He passed these methods on to his apprentices, one of whom was Daniel Burnap, who in turn had Eli Terry as an apprentice. It was Terry who fulfilled the famous Porter Contract for 4,000 clock movements and is considered the most important name in American clockmaking.

Harland's clocks were usually housed in rather plain cases with frets at the top of the hood that are referred to as 'whale's tails'; hence the name whale's tail (or Norwich) case.

This clock has a solid mahogany case with fretwork above, three spiral finials and glazing at the side of the hood. The arched brass dial has Roman hour and Arabic minute numerals, seconds below 12 o'clock and a large date aperture. The dial centre is engraved with flowers and in the arch is shown the moon phases with 'Thomas Harland, Norwich' engraved above this.

An applied brass plate below the chapter ring is engraved 'Joshua Hall', who was possibly the retailer or first owner of the clock.

Height: 7 ft 5¼ in (2.27 m).

— 17 —

AMERICAN TALL-CASE CLOCK, WITH ELI TERRY 'PORTER CONTRACT' WOODEN MOVEMENT OF 30-HOUR DURATION, 1808–09

Eli Terry (1772–1853) was born in East Windsor, Connecticut, the son of Samuel

17

hands, pendulums and weights to Levi and Edward Porter of Waterbury. Subsequently known as the 'Porter Contract', the order was completed by 1810. It was, of course, only made possible by the complete interchangeability of all the components, something that had not been attempted before and indeed signalled the birth of mass production.

Eli Terry's contract subsequently gave rise to some 200 manufacturers in western Connecticut making hundreds of thousands of clocks annually, all using similar wooden movements to those devised by Terry. This continued until the 1830s, when the ready availability of rolled brass meant that it replaced wood.

The clock shown here has a pine case typical of New England styling at that time. The movement, numbered 2467, would date the clock to 1808–09.

17

and Hildah Burnham Terry. He was apprenticed to Daniel Burnap of East Windsor, and had started work on his own account by 1792. He made tools for the manufacture of wooden clocks in quantity using water-powered saws, and in 1797 he patented a clock showing mean and solar time, the first of his many inventions (another was a machine for cutting gear wheels). Among his many achievements was the design of a movement for a wall clock that would run for 30 hours on a 20 in (51 cm) fall of the weight. This was a development that made the production of shelf clocks, which were considerably cheaper than longcase clocks, possible.

Eli Terry entered into what was probably the most significant contract in manufacturing history in 1806, when he undertook a commission to deliver 4,000 30-hour wooden movements, dials,

The Dutch Longcase Clock
· · · · · ·

The production of longcase clocks started in The Netherlands, as in England, fairly shortly after the invention of the pendulum. These early clocks usually had a walnut case of simple, pleasing proportions resting on bun feet and were 7 ft (2.13 m) or less in height, employed spiral twist columns to the hood and were surmounted by carved decoration that was frequently quite elaborate. The square dial of these clocks often had an iron, velvet-covered plate onto which the raised chapter ring and spandrels were applied. To contrast with the black velvet, ornamental gilt-brass hands were used. By the end of the first quarter of the 18th century the arched dial had been adopted, often with moon phases, and clocks had become much taller and frequently employed a bombé base.

Dutch striking, in which the clock strikes out the hours in full both at the halves on a high bell and at the hour on a lower tuned bell, was usually a feature of these longcases' design, and an alarm was frequently incorporated. Musical clocks were made in appreciable numbers. They were usually tall and often quite complex clocks, for instance, with large apertures in the centre of the dial for the days of the week and the months of the year, which were represented by paintings or engravings of the deities and zodiacal signs. A characteristic feature of many of the most elaborate clocks, anything up to 10 to 11 ft (3 to 3.35 m) tall, was the mounting on the top of the case of one or more figures, the most common being Atlas supporting the world.

Whereas in England the popularity and production of longcase clocks rapidly increased as the 18th century progressed, in The Netherlands the numbers made relative to wall clocks, which were in much greater demand, gradually declined.

— **18** —

DUTCH LONGCASE CLOCK, JAN VAN DER SWELLING, LEIDEN, C1770

This Dutch longcase clock is of a style usually made in Amsterdam during the 18th century; however it was made by Jan van der Swelling of Leiden, *c*1770. The fine-quality case, like most 'rich' Amsterdam clocks, is veneered in burr walnut and has inlay and carving. The lenticle is overlaid with a figure of Chronos and on top are typical Dutch finials: two angels on either side and Atlas carrying the world in the centre.

The fine dial of this clock has hour, minute and seconds hands. Apertures display the moon's phases, day, date and month. Painted scenes recessed below the main dial show ships that rock to and fro and St George slaying the dragon.

The movement strikes the quarters on two bells, is provided with an alarm and has Dutch striking, that is, it strikes the hour in full at the hour on a low bell and then repeats the full strike on the half hour on a high bell.

English Bracket Clocks

The term bracket clock, although the one in general use, is somewhat confusing, in that the vast majority of such clocks never rested on a bracket, but were far more likely to have been placed on a table, sideboard or mantelpiece. An alternative name (and that probably most used in the 17th century) is spring clock, however that term now could equally apply, for instance, to spring-driven wall clocks.

Bracket clocks, like longcase clocks, started to be made shortly after the invention of the pendulum. However, whereas the longcase clock rapidly adopted (*c*1675) the anchor escapement, with the benefit of being able to use a long seconds-beating pendulum, the anchor escapement was of far less advantage with the bracket clock – and indeed had one positive disadvantage in that it made the escapement far more critical and the clock more difficult to set up. This was of little importance with the longcase clock, but with a bracket clock, which many would consider portable, it was a major factor. Clocks with verge escapements are far more tolerant of being off-level and thus out of beat. It was only around 1800 that the changeover from verge to anchor escapement took place on this type of clock.

The earlier bracket clocks, as with the longcases, were architectural in style and ebonized. By the 1670s a few were veneered in walnut or olivewood, but ebony still predominated. Because of their small size, the clocks seldom featured marquetry.

— ❶ —

TABLE CLOCK,
ROBERT SEIGNIOR,
LONDON, C1675

Early spring-driven table clocks were architectural in style and usually veneered in ebony or occasionally walnut or olivewood. They bore a close resemblance to contemporary longcase clocks with brass-capped pillars at the four corners. Note the delicate spandrels and the skeletonized chapter ring on this example of a quarter-striking clock.

— ❷ —

SPRING CLOCK, JOHN DREW,
LONDON, LATE 17TH CENTURY

This small and fine ebony-veneered spring clock is by John Drew, who was apprenticed to Joseph Knibb in 1676 and became a Freeman of The Worshipful Company of Clockmakers in 1684. The influence of Knibb is immediately apparent in the proportions and the style of the case, although the shape of the caddy top with applied frets possibly owes more to Thomas Tompion. It is surmounted by a carrying handle, has four small finials, fire-gilt frets at the top of the front door and the sides of the case, and rests on flat bun feet.

The glazed sides and back door reveal the beautifully executed twin fusee movement, which has a finely engraved backplate bearing John Drew's signature in a cartouche. A large countwheel is mounted externally to the backplate; this is numbered so that one can see the last hour that has been struck. The 6 in (15 cm) square brass dial has cherub spandrels with engraving between and a raised chapter ring with half-hour marks.

Height: 14 in (35.5 cm).

SPRING CLOCK, ROBERT HALSTED, LONDON

This fine ebony-veneered spring clock is by Robert Halsted, an eminent maker who was apprenticed to Richard Nau in 1662 and turned over to Isaac Daniell. He became a Freeman of The Clock-makers Company on 6 July 1668 and rose to become Master of the Company in 1699. His signature is found on the clock's backplate.

The two-train movement has verge escapement, pull quarter repeat on three bells, a well-engraved backplate, a back cock cover and that most attractive feature, external clickwork. The 7 in (18 cm) square dial has a raised chapter ring and spandrels (corner pieces), ringed winding holes, a date aperture below 12 o'clock and strike/silent regulation by the 9 o'clock position.

The ebony-veneered case has a well-executed repoussé basket top decorated with cherubs and surmounted by an attractive carrying handle. There are turned finials on the four corners and brass bun feet. The sides are glazed, and there are ornate escutcheons on either side of the front door.

Height: 15 in (38 cm).

— 4 —

BRACKET CLOCK, ANDREW DICKIE, EDINBURGH, 1736-52

The vast majority of bracket clocks made prior to 1750 were produced in London. Even up until the turn of the century the percentage of London-made examples was relatively high.

One place outside London where particularly fine clocks were made was Edinburgh. Seen here is a rare clock with grande-sonnerie striking on six bells, ie, at each quarter it chimes and then strikes out the last hour. The inverted-bell top seen here preceded the bell top, an example of which is seen on page 40.

The backplate is beautifully engraved, the bottom corners are flared out and rising from the corners are thistles (the emblem of Scotland) on which two birds rest. In the bottom centre a vase is depicted, and emanating from this are various flowers spreading over the whole of the backplate. They are so devised that they incorporate all the major arbors and screws, which in effect become the centres of the flowers.

Height: 21 in (53.3 cm).

— **5** —

LACQUERED TABLE CLOCK, JAMES BOYCE, LONDON, LATE 17TH – EARLY 18TH CENTURY

Although the vast majority of lacquer clocks produced were longcases, this form of decoration was also applied to bracket clocks. Black and red were the colours most often used, with red particularly popular on later pieces.

This impressive black-lacquered table clock, of a lovely warm colour, is by James Boyce of London, who started work around 1685 and was a member of The Clockmakers Company from 1692 to 1712. Among the clocks he is recorded as having made is a silver-mounted bracket clock. The lacquer work is of great delicacy, and the quality and depth of the raised work on this clock are especially fine.

The caddy top, which is surrounded by four finials with a fifth one on top, has raised oak leaves applied to the four corners and on the front and back are buildings, trees, foliage, a man and a bird flying overhead. The sides are also decorated with birds. The rest of the case is similarly embellished with several dif-

ferent types of birds and oak leaves applied to the four corners of the front and back doors. A lovely feature of the case is that it is as attractively decorated on the back as it is on the front. The sides of the case are glazed, with carrying handles mounted above, and the clock rests on lion's-paw feet.

The movement has a verge escapement and pull quarter repeat on four bells, which may be activated from either side. The backplate has well-executed floral

engraving, with a wheat-ear design on the border that extends to the edge of the dial. This has strike/silent regulation at 12 o'clock, ringed winding holes, a date aperture above 6 o'clock with a cartouche around it and a further aperture for the mock bob. There are cherub spandrels in the four corners and a raised chapter ring with half-hour and 2½-minute divisions with quartering on its inner edge.

Height: 19½ in (49.5 cm).

— ❻ —

BRACKET CLOCK,

WILLIAM WEBSTER,

LONDON, C1775

William Webster II was undoubtedly one of the finest clockmakers of the second half of the 18th century. The son of a famous father who was Thomas Tompion's journeyman, the younger Webster became a Freeman of The Clockmakers Company in 1734 and by 1755 had risen to become Master. He continued as Liveryman of the Company until 1776.

By the reign of George III ebonized bracket clocks had largely gone out of fashion in favour of those veneered in mahogany. This particular George III bracket clock is of excellent proportions and typical of the best being produced at that time, with a beautifully figured mahogany case of good patination. The bell-shaped top has a carrying handle and is surrounded by four finials; the sides and back are glazed, and the clock rests on brass bracket feet. There is a brass mould on either side of the front door, which has brass-bound frets at the top corners and a brass mould on the clock's inner aspect.

The clock's twin fusee movement has six pillars, verge escapement and a finely engraved backplate bearing Webster's signature. The movement strikes and repeats the hours on a bell. The brass dial has a raised narrow chapter ring, rococo spandrels, strike/silent regulation in the arch and a date aperture.

Height: 20 in (50.8 cm)

— **7** —

BRACKET CLOCK,
LATE 18TH CENTURY

Although case styles in London throughout most of the 18th century were standardized, occasionally a new design would appear. A typical example is this brassmounted, two-train verge bracket clock. Much in the style favoured by Ellicott, *c*1780, the unsigned ebonized clock features a circular convex enamelled dial, and strikes and repeats on a bell. It has a well-engraved backplate and a centre-sweep date hand. The back door and sides are glazed, the latter having a brass bezel around them. The inverted-bell top is surmounted by a carrying handle, and there is a fully opening front door.

Height: 15 in (38 cm).

— **8** —

BRACKET CLOCK,
·
EARDLEY NORTON, LONDON,

LATE 18TH CENTURY

The breakarch-topped case, as seen here, started being produced in the 1770s, the earlier examples tending to be a little shorter and wider. The style was used both with the breakarch dial – in brass on the earlier clocks and on the later ones painted – and also with a circular dial, either painted or silvered brass. A carrying handle was employed on top; this rested on a wooden pad, often brass bound, and sometimes additional pads were placed on either side. Whereas the earlier clocks had a full-width-opening front door, the later examples merely had the dial bezel hinged.

The clock here, by the eminent London maker Eardley Norton, is numbered 2715 on both the dial and backplate. The twin fusee movement with verge escapement has an attractive engraved floral backplate. The brass dial has strike/silent regulation, a raised chapter ring with centre-sweep blued-steel minute and hour hands, and a brass hand for indicating the date.

Height: 18¼ in (47.6 cm)

— **9** —

MUSICAL CLOCK,

ADAM TRAVERS,

LIVERPOOL, C1790

Musical clocks were particularly fashionable in the last quarter of the 18th century, many being exported to the Middle and Far East by eminent makers such as James Cox, Francis Perigal, Eardley Norton and Henry Borrell. They were frequently large and very decorative pieces, and the finest featured automata, ie, figures that moved with the music or as the clock beats. Seen here is a truly magnificent musical bracket clock signed on the recessed plaque in the dial centre below 12 o'clock by Adams Travers, Liverpool, who is recorded as working in that northern city from 1769 to 1777 and in London from 1781 to 1799.

The bell-top case has been made with the very finest mahogany veneers. It is surmounted by a central finial with frets on either side and there are finials at the four corners. The base is brass bound and has rococo feet; there are carrying handles on the sides that are glazed with mirrors, and the four corners of the case are canted and decorated with caryatids.

The 12-tune musical movement is superb. It has a verge escapement, engraved backplate and a large pin barrel running parallel to the plates and extending the full width of the clock. Twenty-five bells are employed with 13 hammers to play one of 6 tunes at each hour.

The brass dial has a raised chapter ring and spandrels; date aperture above 6 o'clock; strike/silent and music/silent at the top corners, and the names of 12 tunes listed out around the arch. In this is a beautifully executed parlour scene with seven minstrels playing various instruments; four of these are automata, that is, they move their arms, bows etc as the clock beats. A most attractive feature – and an indication of the thought put into the design of the dial – is that the tune-selector hand is kept short, so as not to overlap the picture, and reads off against a small dial numbered from 1 to 6 in the dial centre.

Height: 27 in (68.6 cm).

— ⑩ —

**MAHOGANY BRACKET CLOCK,
JOHN WAYLETT,
LONDON, C1785**

By around 1780 the brass dial started to give way to the painted dial, and by 1800 this process was almost complete. Whereas the earlier painted dials often followed the breakarch shape of the brass dials, this was gradually dropped in favour of the circular dial, although the basic design of the clock's case remained the same.

Seen here is a painted-dial bracket clock by John Waylett. At this stage it still retains the verge escapement and an engraved backplate. Note the use of decorative brass frets below the dial.

By 1675–80 the architectural style started to give way to the caddy top, sometimes left plain and sometimes decorated with fretted and gilt-brass mounts. By 1685–90 the fretted-out gilt-brass basket top was being employed. Often this was cast, but more frequently the designs featured on it were created by repoussé (beaten out) work. The earliest of these were relatively small and shallow, but gradually they got larger and more elaborate. Indeed, by 1710 a double-basket top was often being employed. The majority of these clocks were ebony-veneered, with only the rare model finished in walnut, olivewood or other similar kinds of woods.

By 1712–15 the breakarch dial was coming into fashion, and in its early stages it was sometimes relatively shallow. The caddy top gradually gave way to the inverted bell, a style that was to persist until the mid 18th century. Again, the vast majority of these clocks were black, but they were usually now veneered in ebonized fruitwood rather than ebony. Bracket clocks were also decorated in lacquer, but less frequently than the longcase clocks of the time. By the 1760s the inverted-bell top started to be superseded by the bell top, and other case designs evolved. It was at this stage that mahogany became the favourite wood for bracket-clock cases.

Up until this time the brass dial incorporating a raised chapter ring and spandrels had always been employed, but by the 1770s the allover engraved and silvered brass dial was seen quite frequently. The painted or white dial also became increasingly popular from *c*1780 onward, but it was usually left plain with no decoration at the corners. This was probably largely because the vast majority of bracket clocks being produced at the time – and indeed throughout the last half of the 17th and the 18th centuries – originated in London. It was principally only in the country that white dials carried coloured decoration, although this is by no means always true. Examples of this are the beautiful scenes that are sometimes depicted in the arch of musical bracket clocks featuring automata, such as people playing musical instruments, sawing logs and suchlike.

By the 1800s painted, and occasionally silvered-brass, dials were being used almost universally on bracket clocks. The earlier ones – usually just prior to 1800 – were breakarch in form, but after this time they were generally circular.

— ⑪ —

**MAHOGANY CLOCK,
THOMAS GADSBY,
LEICESTER, C1830**

By the 1820s brass frets were seldom seen below the dial and clocks had become a little taller and narrower. The break at the side of the arch was now far less pronounced and indeed was sometimes omitted. Whereas the earlier clocks had a full-width-opening front door, after *c*1810 just the brass bezel is hinged.

This well-figured mahogany twin fusee clock strikes and repeats the hours on a bell. It has a 7 in (18 cm) convex painted dial with Roman numerals and employs an anchor escapement. The breakarch case is surmounted by a handle that rests on a brass-bound mahogany pad. There is brass inlay at the front of the case and fish-scale frets in the sides.

Height: 14½ in (37 cm).

— ⑫ —

CHAMFER-TOPPED
BRACKET CLOCK,
WILLIAM CRIBB, LONDON, C1820

A distinctive case style that evolved at the beginning of the 19th century was the chamfer-topped bracket clock, a typical example of which is seen here. They were usually veneered in well-figured rosewood or mahogany and in some instances were inlaid with brass. In many cases a brass pineapple finial was placed on top and sometimes the top of the case was fluted.

This bracket clock by Cribb is a lovely faded colour and is extensively inlaid with brass over the whole of the front of the case. The corners are chamfered and inlaid with brass, the sides have brass fretwork and ringed carrying handles, and the piece rests on ball feet. The twin fusee movement, which strikes and repeats on a bell, has shaped plates and an 8 in (20 cm) convex circular dial.

Height: 17 in (43 cm).

— **13** —

'FOUR GLASS' CLOCK, EARLY 19TH CENTURY

A distinctive case style that appeared early in the 19th century was the 'four glass' type, which has glass on all four sides. This was undoubtedly stimulated by the arrival on the scene of the carriage clock. Sometimes they had a carrying handle on top, but more frequently this feature was omitted. Similarly, a pendulum was probably generally favoured and would have been provided with a clamp, al-though when it was likely that the clock would be used for travelling a balance wheel escapement was employed.

An attractive feature of these clocks was their relatively small size, such as that of the one illustrated (a height of 9 in/23 cm was common). The clocks were finished in handsome woods such as satinwood, mahogany, rosewood or walnut. The dials were generally of engraved and silvered brass but painted dials were also used, particularly on the later pieces.

Several new case styles evolved during the Regency period, examples of which are seen on pages 45 and 46. These persisted in gradually modified forms until the middle of the century and often incorporated inlaid brass. During the Victorian and Edwardian eras clocks tended to be larger and more heavily decorated, sometimes with carving, and initially the white dial predominated. However, from *c*1870 onward, reproductions of Georgian clocks became popular, copying their predecessors' style but sometimes being smaller and quite frequently much larger. In the latter cases it was to provide space to accommodate a nest of bells or gongs to allow quarter-chiming, which had become extremely popular following the completion of the great clock at Westminster now generally known as Big Ben.

As the century progressed, chiming increasingly was provided by a series of coiled gongs, four for Westminster – by far the most popular – and eight for other chimes, such as St Michael. Gongs were also used more and more for the hour strike, even when bells were used for the quarters. Probably the ultimate was the clock that produced one or two different tunes on eight or sometimes even nine or ten bells, and could also provide Westminster chimes on four gongs with a gong for the hour. As a further throwback to the Georgian era, these clocks usually – but by no means always – had a brass dial and sometimes an engraved backplate.

By the early 20th century the production of clocks such as those mentioned and, indeed, most bracket clocks had virtually ceased in the United Kingdom. They were largely superseded by the smaller and cheaper French and German copies of earlier English bracket clock styles and also by the very decorative French mantel clocks.

BRACKET CLOCK, 1880

By the 1850s much larger bracket clocks were becoming popular; these frequently chimed the quarters on four or eight bells or gongs. Their production was undoubtedly stimulated in large measure by the completion of the clock now known as Big Ben for the Palace of Westminster in 1859. The majority of these clocks were ebonized and embellished with extensive ormolu mounts, but others were veneered in mahogany or rosewood. Seen here is a superb Victorian triple-chain fusee bracket clock quarter-chiming on four gongs or eight bells. It has a brass dial with a raised chapter ring, cherub spandrels and regulation for fast/slow, chime/silent and chime on eight bells or Westminster chime.

The well-figured rosewood case is extensively inlaid with brass and has fluted brass columns and brass frets on either side. It is surmounted by five brass finials and rests on fluted brass feet.

Height: 31 in (79 cm).

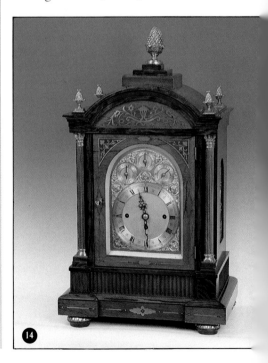

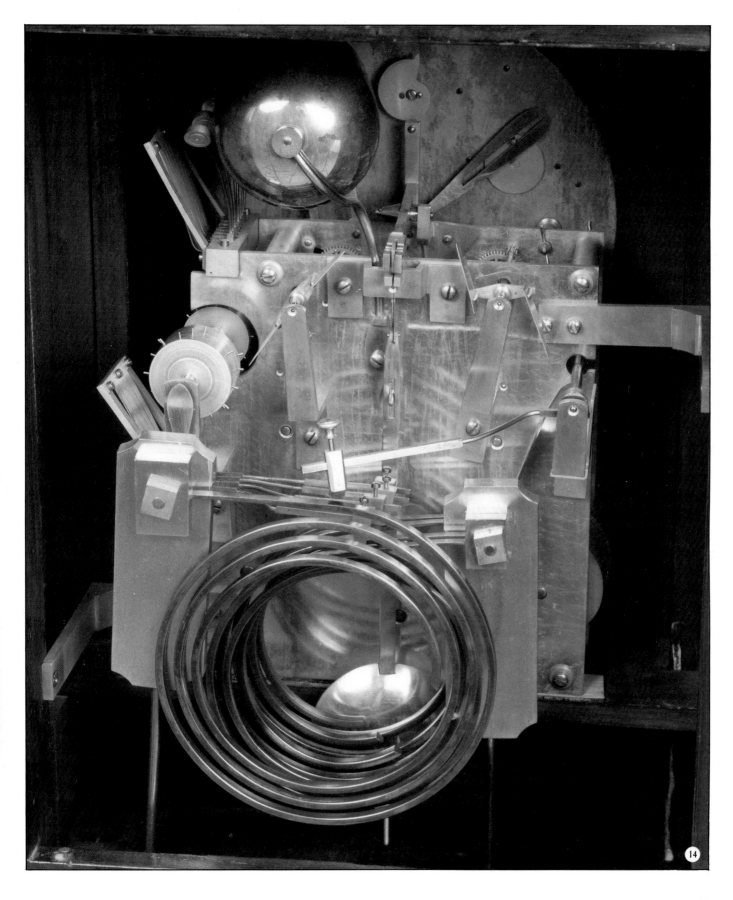

French Mantel Clocks

The approach to clockmaking in France in the last half of the 17th and the 18th centuries was vastly different to that in England. Except for those made in the very early period, the clocks were far more ornate (in order to match French furniture), and indeed this aspect of their design was usually the dominant factor.

Whereas in England the production of clocks usually only required two craftsmen, the clockmaker and the cabinetmaker, in France far more people were involved. For instance, a sculptor, caster, chaser, engraver, gilder, enameller and porcelain manufacturer might all contribute to a clock's creation. The better clocks were considered works of art, and many fine artists were employed, for instance, to produce the patterns for the mounts applied to the case or even, in some instances, the whole case. This is scarcely surprising in a country that produced the best bronzes in the world, most of whose subjects came from mythology. The decoration applied to the cases varied. Tortoiseshell was used extensively either on its own or in conjunction with inlaid brass (this was called Boulle work, after the inventor of the process). Silver was also let into the tortoiseshell. Horn was sometimes used as a veneer, and it was usually stained green.

Other methods favoured to decorate cases and increase their richness included the use of exotic woods such as tulipwood and kingwood, frequently laid out in geometric designs, and the widespread employment of marquetry and parquetry.

Beautifully conceived and executed porcelain clocks were produced quite early on in the 18th century. The cases were often imported from famous factories such as Meissen and Dresden and frequently comprised flowers and figures of young girls.

Fine bronze models of animals – for instance, lions, elephants and horses – were used, carrying the clock itself on their back, and the figure of Chronos also appeared, with the clock under his arm.

— **1** —

MANTEL CLOCK,
LATE 18TH CENTURY

Astronomy reading a book, with another volume at her feet, is depicted on this particularly fine quality late-18th-century French fire-gilt and bronze mantel clock. The allegorical figure is further surrounded by Cupid, a globe and various astronomical instruments. The whole rests on an attractively flecked grey marble base, which is supported by four turned and gilded brass feet. The substantial movement strikes on a bell, employing an external countwheel, and has silk suspension. The well-executed 5½ in (14 cm) convex enamelled dial, which is signed 'Lepaute De Bellefontaine', has Roman hour numerals and Arabic minute numerals. There is a little gilt star at each of the five-minute marks.

Height: 19½ in (49.5 cm).

— **2** —

CHRONOS CLOCK,
RADENT, PARIS, C1820

A very finely executed and well-patinated figure of the winged god Chronos (Father Time) carries a scythe in one arm and a clock beneath the other. The two-train movement, which strikes the hours and halves on a bell, employs a countwheel and has silk suspension.

The gilded dial, which features black Roman numerals, is beautifully decorated with engine turning and has a gilded bezel in the form of a serpent holding its own tail. It is signed 'Radent, Paris' and dates from about 1820. The figure rests on a rouge marble base that is supported by four bronze eagle feet.

Height: 20½ in (52 cm).

French and Swiss Wall Clocks

The French produced two main types of wall clock in the 18th and 19th centuries, both of which they termed cartel clocks. However, here, this description is usually reserved for decorative wall clocks, such as that seen on page 53. The second group is described – at least when referring to English clocks – as a bracket clock on bracket, as the two components are usually entirely separate from each other. Several terms seem to be used in France for the bracket on which the clock rests, such as *soubassement, console, support* or *cul de lampe.* The word *socle* is also sometimes used, but is possibly best confined to the plinth or pillar on which the clock rests.

Cartel Clocks

Cartel clocks, nearly always of fire-gilt bronze and usually beautifully chased and decorated, started to be produced quite early in the 18th century. The first clocks had fairly substantial movements with rectangular plates, silk suspension, verge escapements and fine convex enamelled dials; they were frequently signed both on this and the backplate.

These clocks continued to be made in gradually changing form, but usually as fairly substantial clocks until the beginning of the 19th century. It was at this stage that the mass production of French clock movements – still of fine quality, however – started in earnest. These were smaller than their predecessors and employed circular plates, usually with anchor escapements and either countwheel or rack strike. The earlier examples tended to use silk suspension.

The clocks now became, on average, much smaller in size. They maintained their popularity throughout the 19th century, although the number produced was far less than mantel clocks, and indeed they were still being made up until the outbreak of World War I.

Bracket Clock on Bracket

· · · · · ·

These clocks started to be produced at the beginning of the 18th century and were usually – but by no means always – large clocks anything up to 5 ft (1.52 m) in overall length. The clock and its accompanying bracket, although separate, were always conceived as one overall design, usually highly decorative. The pendulum was frequently visible and the dial made up with an ornamental background on which raised enamelled numerals were placed.

Probably the most common decoration applied to the case was Boulle marquetry, that is, delicate designs in brass let into a tortoiseshell background. Tortoiseshell alone, usually brown or green, was also used, in conjunction with ormolu mounts as well as lacquer decoration.

— ❶ —

GILT-BRONZE CARTEL CLOCK,

MARTINET,

EARLY 18TH CENTURY

This French timepiece of fire-gilt bronze features a convex enamelled dial, verge escapement and pull quarter repeat on two bells. Interestingly, it is signed 'London' on the dial, and this is probably because part of the Martinet family came to England as refugees in the early part of the eighteenth century. However, the clock would actually have been manufactured in France.

2

— 2 —

LOUIS XV ORMOLU QUARTER-REPEATING CARTEL TIMEPIECE, C1745

This is signed on the convex enamelled dial 'Jean Baptiste Baillon', and the signature is repeated on the backplate of the movement, together with the number 408. It employs a form of anchor escapement with divided but interlinked pallets devised by Antoine Thiout in the 1730s. The clock has baluster pillars and repeats the quarters on two bells.

The case is composed of shells and billowing clouds, with a maiden above and two winged putti below. As is usual, the quality of finish of the case, as well as the execution of the dial, is excellent.

Length: 22 in (56 cm).

— 3 —

MUSICAL CLOCK, JACQUET DROZ, C1770

A fine red Boulle *pendule* complete with original bracket, this was once in the Palais Esterhazy in Vienna. It is signed 'Pierre Jacquet Droz, à La Chaux de Fonds', probably the most eminent of all Swiss clockmakers. He specialized in musical clocks, including those incorporating singing birds.

The case and bracket have fine ormolu mounts, and the convex enamelled dial has Roman hour numerals and Arabic minute numerals.

The main movement chimes the quarters and strikes the hour on bells; below this is a massive musical movement that plays at the hour or at will on flutes.

3

Dutch Wall Clocks

I n England the longcase was to dominate clock production since the invention of the pendulum in 1657, but in The Netherlands the simple rectangular wall clock, hung from the wall by two eyelets, first appeared on the scene. These were called Hague clocks, and the earliest examples were usually just timepieces, that is, they had no strike. Interestingly, probably because Christiaan Huygens, who invented the pendulum, visited Paris regularly, clocks very similar to Hague clocks appeared in the French capital at almost the same time as they appeared in The Netherlands.

As the century progressed these clocks gradually became more ornate. They were either spring- or weight-driven; of single- or eight-day duration; and strike work and an alarm were often provided. Silk suspension was employed for the pendulum, and the dial usually consisted of a velvet-covered cast-iron plate on which the silver or silvered chapter ring was mounted, sometimes solid and sometimes fretted out.

— ❶ —

HAGUE CLOCK,
SALOMON COSTER, C1660

The first pendulum clocks to be made in The Netherlands were the so-called Hague clocks, of which the one shown here, by Salomon Coster, c1660, is a typical example. It has a simple rectangular case with a double door, the first glazed to protect the dial that is opened for winding and a second one on which the movement is mounted. There are two eyelets on top for hanging it on a wall.

The simple spring-driven movement has a bob pendulum and cycloidal cheeks at the top to try and keep the pendulum oscillating in a constant time no matter how wide its arc of swing.

— ❷ —

STOELKLOK, C1740

This clock would have been made in Friesland in the northeastern part of the country around 1740. It has so-called 'ears' on either side of the back of the case, and its frets are made of lead.

The movement, which strikes the hours and halves on a bell, employs a verge escapement. It also has an alarm, activated by the additional small weights seen in the photograph.

The stool on which the clock rests has painted decoration; the dial also is painted.

❶

The Stoelklok
· · · · · · ·

The *stoelklok* is basically a clock resting on a wall bracket. This may be either very simple in design, as with the early clocks and similar to that used for lantern clocks, or extremely ornate, as seen on most of the examples produced in the 19th century. The *stoelklok* and the *staartklok* (or tail clock), which is described later, were to dominate Dutch clock production during the late 17th and the 18th centuries, whereas in England the number of wall clocks produced during this period was very small compared to the longcase clock.

The first of the *stoelkloks* produced, examples of which are now rarely seen, employed a balance wheel and verge escapement, but the vast majority made use of a pendulum. The earliest clocks often had a raised chapter ring laid on a plain background, but within a short period the entire dial became decorated with painted scenes.

Although the first examples of these clocks were made in or around Amsterdam, their production rapidly spread throughout much of the country, where distinct regional characteristics soon developed. In the later period, iron or lead decoration was added to the clocks, for instance, in the form of cherubs, female figures or animals. Painted wooden figures, usually mermaids, were added to either side of the bracket at the back.

The Staartklok
· · · · · · ·

The *staartklok* is really a hooded wall clock and indeed probably evolved from the earliest of these produced in either England or The Netherlands. However, their characteristic feature is the extension of the bracket down below the clock – so as, in effect, to provide a box to protect the pendulum. This box, as on the early longcases, usually has a glazed aperture, often overlaid with decorative fretted-out gilded brass.

The early clocks tended to be fairly simple in concept and the dials similar to those used on longcase clocks at that time. On later clocks the dial was painted. The clocks are normally of 30-hour duration and employ exposed brass cased weights. The majority are fairly large clocks, usually with a seconds-beating pendulum, but much smaller versions were made occasionally. The finish of the cases varied appreciably. Sometimes they were of simple oak, but they were also painted, carved and had marquetry let into them. As with the *stoelklok,* strong regional characteristics rapidly developed.

— **3** —

STOELKLOK, C1800

A typical Dutch *stoelklok* (above, top and bottom right), this features mermaids on either side at the back and cherubs on each side of the dial. Note the very ornate nature of the movement, with attractively turned vertical and horizontal pillars and verge escapement. It is of 30-hour duration and has an alarm.

— **4** —

STAARTKLOK, C1840

Staartkloks of this style (far right) were made in Friesland in the first half of the 19th century. Note the original top finials with trumpeters on either side and Atlas carrying the world on his shoulders in the centre. It is of 30-hour duration, strikes the hours in full and halves in passing, and is provided with an alarm. There is an anchor escapement.

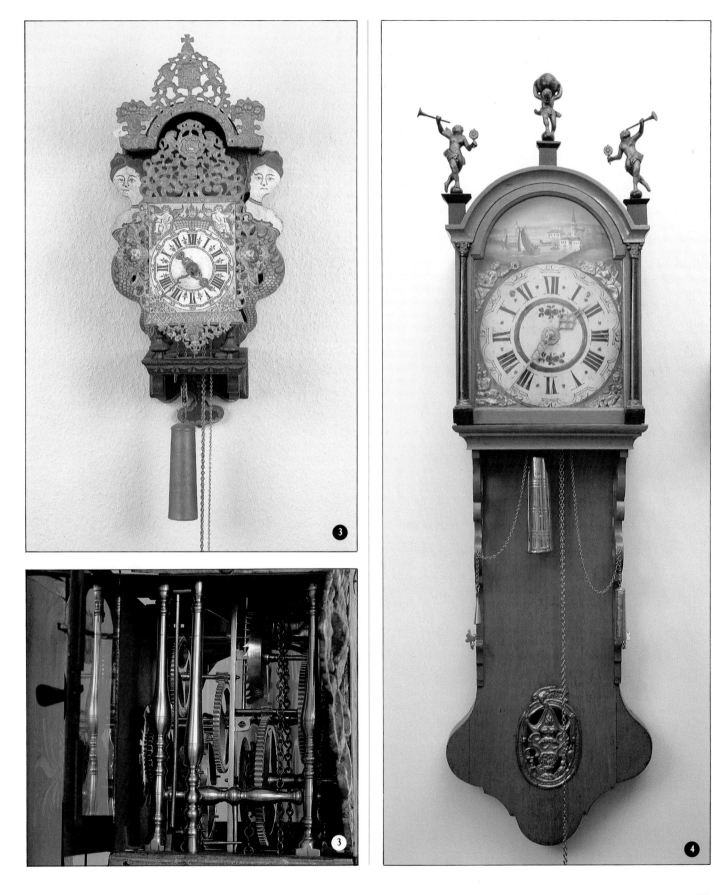

English Wall Clocks

The lantern was undoubtedly the earliest wall clock, first appearing in Europe, particularly southern Germany and northern Italy around 1500, with production starting in England some 100 years later. These were sometimes hung on the wall by means of a hoop extending backward from the top plate of the movement and engaging on a suitable hook. At the same time spikes fixed to the rear of the back feet were pushed into the wall to keep the clock vertical and stop it moving while it was being wound. From this is derived the term 'hoop and spikes'. Alternatively, a bracket, usually of oak, was fixed to the wall and the clock placed on this.

The first lantern clocks made in Germany employed a verge escapement with a foliot, but this gradually gave way to the balance wheel, which was used on virtually all early English lantern clocks.

With the discovery of the pendulum in 1657 the balance wheel became obsolete. Most of the clocks that had been made with a balance wheel were converted so as to employ the pendulum, which ensured far better timekeeping.

Some 12 years later the anchor escapement, usually employed with the 39 in (1 m) seconds-beating pendulum, was invented, possibly by Clement. However, whereas with the longcase the changeover from verge to anchor escapement was almost instantaneous, with the lantern clock it only gradually occurred, over a period of maybe 30 to 40 years. This was in part because the lantern, being a relatively simple and inexpensive clock with only an hour hand, was never expected to keep particularly good time.

By 1710–20 the heyday of the lantern clock had passed. The lantern clock was almost completely supplanted by the longcase clock, particularly the 30-hour type, although its production never completely ceased in the 18th century.

— ❶ —

**VERGE LANTERN CLOCK,
THOMAS PALMER, SHEFFORD,
LATE 17TH CENTURY**

This lantern clock has a short bob pendulum with a verge escapement that is typical of those produced in the last half of the 17th century. Note the chunky construction of the movement with vertical strips of brass, fixed to the top and bottom plates, which carry the arbors. The ropes for the weights driving the time and strike trains may be seen, one behind the other, at the bottom of the movement. The attractive clock dial is decorated profusely in the centre with tulips and signed in a plaque below 12 o'clock by Thomas Palmer of Shefford, Bedfordshire, who worked around 1690. The chapter ring has quartering on its inner edge and attractive half-hour markings. The movement has heavy arbors, some of which are tapered, and the verge rests on a knife edge and has a fixed bob pendulum. The dolphin frets on top of the clock are typical of those used on lantern clocks during this period.

Height: 15 in (38 cm).

— **2** —

LANTERN CLOCK, GEORGE THATCHER, CRANBROOK, 18TH CENTURY

By around 1700 the majority of lantern clocks employed the anchor escapement together with a long pendulum, some-times but not always seconds-beating. Many of the clocks were fixed to the wall by a hoop attached to the top plate of the movement together with spikes fitted into the back of the rear ball feet. However, in other cases a simple oak bracket such as the one seen here was employed.

This clock, by George Thatcher of Cranbrook, would have been made in the first half of the 18th century. It has an engraved fret at the front and plain ones at the sides. The dial centre has floral engraving, and there is a raised chapter ring with half-hour divisions and quartering on the inner aspect. This is now of polished brass but originally would probably have been silvered. An anchor escapement is used with a seconds-beating pendulum (because of its length it cannot be seen here). This lantern is quite rare, in that it is fitted with a rack as opposed to the usual countwheel strike. The bracket is a later copy.

Height: clock only/with brackets: 15 in/24 in (38 cm/61 cm).

— **3** —

ALARM AND WINGED LANTERN
CLOCKS, EARLY 18TH CENTURY

The fitting of a weight-driven alarm to lantern clocks was quite common, right from the earliest days, but had largely gone out of favour by 1700. Seen here are two lantern clocks, both fitted with a central disc for setting the time for the alarm to go off. The actual mechanism for the alarm was usually mounted on the backplate, the bell on top being struck repeatedly by a bar that swung to and fro inside the bell.

The winged lantern clock is a most attractive variant of the standard verge lantern. Instead of being mounted at the back of the clock, the pendulum is situated in the centre between the striking and time sides of the movement. The bob consists of a curved strip of brass with an arrow on either end. As this swings to and fro, the arrows appear and disappear on either side, being visible through two glazed winged extensions.

— **4** —

WEIGHT-DRIVEN LANTERN CLOCK CONVERTED TO SPRING, BARNARD DAMMANT, COLCHESTER, EARLY 18TH CENTURY

The weight-driven lantern clock was somewhat difficult to accommodate, in that allowance had to be made for the long pendulum and somewhat unsightly weights and rope that hung down below the clock. Thus when reproduction lantern clocks started to be made in the mid 19th century, they included a spring-driven movement and a short pendulum that was concealed within the case. In this way they could be placed on a table or mantelpiece.

At the same time, many of the older lantern clocks were converted from weight- to spring-driven movements with a short pendulum. Just such a clock, made early in the 18th century by Barnard Dammant of Colchester, is seen here. Dolphin frets are used, the front one being engraved, and this has the usual bell strap and bell with a decorative finial. The dial is engraved in the centre and has a raised chapter ring with half-hour divisions and quartering on its inner aspect. It is now fitted with a two-train chain fusee movement, the immediate giveaway being the winding holes that have been cut in the dial.

Hooded Wall Clocks
· · · · · · ·

The hooded wall clock, an attractive alternative to the lantern clock, was produced – in limited numbers only – from the late 17th to the end of the 18th century. The earlier examples usually had simple 30-hour movements with a single-handed brass dial anything from 5–10 in (13–25 cm) square. In effect they rested on a bracket and were protected by a hood that slid off this. On the London clocks this may well have been veneered in walnut or mahogany, but on the country clocks solid oak was the timber of choice.

As the century passed, the breakarch dial came into fashion, and a minute and sometimes a seconds hand were also provided. By 1780 the painted dial was being used increasingly, but by 1800 the production of hooded wall clocks had largely ceased.

The Tavern, or Act of Parliament, Clock
· · · · · · ·

The terms 'tavern' and 'Act of Parliament' tend to be used synonymously to describe large weight-driven wall clocks, usually with black-lacquered cases. This usage is not correct, however, as tavern clocks were made from 1730–35 onward, whereas the Act of Parliament that gave the clocks their name was not introduced until 1797. It imposed a duty of 5 shillings on every clock, 10 shillings on each gold watch and 2 shillings and 6 pence on those made of silver or other metals.

Despite this fact, it would appear that most people hid their clocks and watches to avoid paying and this gave rise to a greatly increased number of large public clocks, usually tavern clocks, by which to tell the time: hence, the alternative name of Act of Parliament clocks. The act produced such a disastrous decline in the demand for watches and clocks that the clockmakers petitioned Parliament and within a year the act was repealed.

The early tavern clocks usually have a square dial with a shallow arch at the top, following the curve of the chapter ring, and below the dial a trunk into which the pendulum and weight extend. The basically square dial gradually evolved into one that was shield-shaped; octagonal dials were also used. The circular dial, either white or black, probably appeared c1760.

By 1780–90 the use of lacquer cases had largely given way to mahogany, and within two decades their production had almost ceased.

**HOODED WALL CLOCK,
JOHN ELLICOTT, C1770**

By the middle of the 18th century the lantern clock was going out of fashion in favour of more decorative clocks. One style that was to evolve – and was used by certain eminent makers such as Ellicott, John Holmes and the partnership of Thomas Mudge and William Dutton – was the hooded wall clock, an excellent example of which is seen here. It has a slide-off hood surmounted by fretwork at the sides and canted front corners. The clock is provided with a slide-off ogee base containing a key drawer.

The five-pillar movement has a verge escapement and a 9½ in (24 cm) engraved and silvered brass dial with the attractive feature that might be termed a flat-topped breakarch. Strike/silent regulation is provided at 3 o'clock.

Overall length, including the finial: 32 in (81 cm).

— **6** —

TAVERN OR ACT OF PARLIAMENT
CLOCK, WILLIAM NASH,
BRIDGE, C1780

By the reign of George II a highly efficient system of coaching existed over much of the country, making regular runs between the major cities and stopping to change horses and pick up passengers at the various coaching inns.

These coaches kept surprisingly accurate time, so it was important for the inns to have accurate clocks that were prominently displayed. Thus was born the tavern clock or Act of Parliament clock (see page 64).

The example seen here is by William Nash of Bridge (Canterbury), who is recorded as working from 1762 to 1794. It has a white-painted dial with black Roman numerals and a substantial wooden surround some 28 in (71 cm) in diameter. The trunk door has a painted scene with a courting couple in the foreground and another young girl behind. The rest of the door, the scroll base and the sides are decorated with bold floral designs in gilt.

The well-made movement has tapering plates and a four-wheel train, that is, it winds anticlockwise. It has an oval lead weight and brass-cased pendulum bob.

Length: 5 ft (1.52 m)

— **7** —

ACT OF PARLIAMENT CLOCK,
THOMAS BENTLEY,
DARLINGTON, C1780

Although the majority of tavern clocks were similar to that seen on page 65, with a circular dial and drop trunk, other variants were produced, such as the shield-shaped clock and the teardrop, an example of which is seen here.

This is a particularly good tavern clock in pristine condition. It has a black 25 in (63.5 cm) circular dial with Roman hour and Arabic minute numerals. Immediately below the dial is the bold signature, 'Thomas Bentley, Darlington', contained in a cartouche. He is recorded as working *c*1776. The trunk door, which is removable, has gilt chinoiserie in the top half and in the lower half a painting of a man carrying a hare, and two dogs and a horse. The movement, which winds anticlockwise, has a rectangular driving weight and brass-faced pendulum bob.

Length: 5 ft 2 in (1.57 m).

— **8** —

TAVERN CLOCK, J IRELAND, LONDON, LATE 18TH CENTURY

This small, attractive green-lacquered tavern clock is signed 'J. Ireland, Maiden Lane, Covent Garden'. At the bottom is the inscription *Bibe, Vel Discede* (Drink Up or Leave), which was obviously designed to stimulate turnover in the pub.

The shaped door, which is removable, is decorated with a country scene of men and women playing with a dog. The movement has tapered plates and winds anticlockwise. Unusually for this type of clock, the 18 in (46 cm) painted wooden dial is protected by a glazed wooden hinged bezel. The hands are brass.

— **9** —

MAHOGANY CASED WALL CLOCKS

Toward the end of the 18th century lacquer started to go out of fashion for the decoration of large wall clocks such as the Act of Parliament. In its place mahogany was largely used. Some of the earlier examples, like that seen on the right by Charles Franken of Bath, c1790, were quite similar, having painted wooden dials that were left unprotected. However, quite early on a front glass contained within a hinged brass bezel was employed, the clock on the left by John Gartly of Aberdeen, c1810 being a good example.

The production of these clocks had largely ceased by the 1820s, although they continued to be made in Norfolk, if in a somewhat different form.

Shown in the centre of the picture is a late-18th-century hooded wall clock with engraved and silvered dial.

Dial Clocks
· · · · · · ·

English cartel clocks, similar to their French brethren but with cases of gilt wood rather than fire-gilt brass, started to appear *c*1730 and continued in production for some 50 years, albeit in only small numbers.

These and the circular black-dial clocks that started to be made at roughly the same time employed spring-driven movements with a verge escapement. Indeed, this form of escapement was to persist on all spring-driven wall clocks until the end of the 18th century.

Some time after the black-dial clock was produced, white-dial clocks, still employing a wooden background, came into fashion; but these were gradually replaced from the 1760s onward by the engraved and silvered brass dial, which was to remain in common use until the early 19th century. From 1780, however, the convex painted dial was to become increasingly fashionable.

From around 1800 the decorative mahogany case became popular, usually employed with a drop trunk that either chamfered or, later, curved back toward the wall. As the Regency period progressed decorative brass inlay was added, and by *c*1830 there was often a glazed brass-bound aperture in the front of the trunk through which the

SILVERED-DIAL WALL CLOCK, LATE 18TH CENTURY

A direct descendant of the cartel clock, the English wall clock with engraved and silvered brass dial probably started to appear around 1770. They were nearly always simple timepieces, that is, without strike, and some of the earlier examples had a cutout in the dial for the mock bob (as did the bracket clocks). Many had decorative engraving and beautifully executed signatures. By the early 1800s, plainer dials with simpler signatures were being produced.

Alongside the silvered-dial clocks, examples with wooden dials were also being made; these probably continued in production for a little longer.

The good late-18th-century English wall clock seen here, with verge escapement and tapering plates to the substantial fusee movement, has a 12 in (30.5 cm) circular silvered-brass dial signed 'Le Grave, London', with a beautifully engraved spray of flowers surrounding the city's name. The substantial and attractively moulded brass bezel extends practically to the edge of the case.

Length: 16 in (41 cm).

— ⓫ —

STRIKING SPRING-DRIVEN WALL CLOCK, THOMAS HAWKINS, LONDON, C1800

Around the turn of the century some particularly fine quality mahogany wall clocks were being produced; these had a trunk below the dial with what is known as a chisel base, as it slopes back to a sharp point at the wall. The vast majority had either painted or silvered-brass dials, but on rare occasions an enamelled dial was employed, as on the clock pictured.

— ⑫ —

**REGENCY DROP-TRUNK WALL
CLOCK, THOMAS BLUNDELL,
LIVERPOOL, C1825**

As the 19th century progressed painted dials became the norm. At first these were convex with a matching convex glass, but later they became flat. The standard diameter was 12 in (30.5 cm) but 10 in (25 cm) and even 8 in (20 cm) are occasionally seen.

The cases gradually became more decorative, with, for instance, the addition of inlay and the application of carved 'ears' at either side. A drop was employed below the trunk, which was curved instead of chiselled as on the earlier clocks, and at a later date a brass-framed glazed aperture was provided through which the pendulum might be seen. By this time the base no longer curved into the wall.

pendulum bob might be seen swinging to and fro. By the middle of the century the convex dial had given way to a flat one.

Throughout the entire 19th century and well into the 20th the simple circular painted-dial, spring-driven fusee wall clock was produced in very large numbers. It was used throughout the country in most public places, such as schools, railway stations and offices, and of course at home. It was also exported all over the world.

Austrian, German and Maltese Wall Clocks

The Vienna Regulator
· · · · · · ·

The term 'Vienna regulator' is somewhat confusing, in that these clocks, which feature a movement with exposed brass cased pendulum bob and usually weights within a fully glazed case, were not always made in Vienna. To understand this it must be remembered that from 1520 to 1918 Austria was part of the Austro-Hungarian Empire, and it is for this reason that clocks made in Austria, Hungary and Czechoslovakia, for instance, often bear such a close resemblance. Vienna, however, was undoubtedly the most important of the imperial courts, and consequently its influence on many things, including clock-making, was the strongest.

During the late 17th and a large part of the 18th centuries, English clockmaking was to have a strong sway on Austrian clockmaking, with designs being copied and movements and even whole clocks being imported. However, in 1780 it was decided to improve the standard of Austria's clock- and watchmaking by inviting some 50 Swiss craftsmen – subsequently increased to 150 – to come and work there. Many of these were specialists – for instance, in dial, bezel, wheel, pinion and file manufacture – and undoubtedly the skills they imparted to their Austrian colleagues provided the foundation for the beautifully executed clocks made in the Austro-Hungarian Empire in the first half of the 19th century.

A further influence on the Viennese was that of the French, which was reinforced by the marriage of Napoleon to Marie Louise of the House of Hapsburg in 1804. This confluence further gave rise to a renewed appreciation of classical proportions – and to the Vienna regulator, which is a perfect example of such classicism. However, there was a big difference between the French and Austro-Hungarian products, in that the latter were much less flamboyant and more delicately constructed than French examples. Undoubtedly this made them much cheaper to produce and so more affordable, but also rendered them far more appealing in many people's eyes.

— ❶ —

EIGHT-DAY LATERNDLUHR
VIENNA REGULATOR,
G J BAUER, C1830

The *laterndluhr* was almost the first style of case to appear in Vienna, *c*1800. Some were roughly 5 ft (1.5 m) long and incorporated a seconds-beating pendulum, but others were smaller, even miniatures only 20–25 in (51–64 cm) long.

This particular clock, which has an ebonized case, is some 35 in (89 cm) long, and has a 6 in (15 cm) gilt two-piece dial with a silver bezel between the two halves and an outer engraved bezel. It is signed 'G. J. Bauer in Wien', and the delicate Roman numerals are painted.

The eight-day movement has a weight-driven time train, and springs are provided for the hours and quarters. This is a relatively common arrangement on early grande-sonnerie striking clocks, but in these instances they are usually of only two-day duration. Dead-beat escapement is used and maintaining power is provided.

— **2** —

VIENNA REGULATORS, 1825—50

Right A *dachluhr* (roof top) case, *c*1825, which would be described as 'six light', that is, it is glazed with six pieces of glass, two on each side, which are divided by a glazing bar. The case is mahogany-veneered and has boxwood stringing. The movement has a wood rod pendulum and is of one-month duration. The dial is 'one piece', that is, it does not have a recessed centre, and there is a delicate engine-turned bezel.

Left An eight-day cherrywood Vienna regulator, also with a six-light case, but with a carved cresting on top instead of the roof top. It has a 'pie-crust' bezel around the dial, which came into favour around 1835–40.

Centre A rare mahogany cased wall clock of three-month duration, with grande-sonnerie striking on gongs and a wood rod pendulum. It has a fine convex enamelled dial with a pie-crust bezel and very delicate hands, the minute being counterbalanced to reduce the power requirement to a minimum.

2

— **3** —

'TWO-PIECE' DIAL CLOCKS, MID 19TH CENTURY

By the 1840s the 'two-piece' dial, ie, with recessed centre, had come into favour.
Left A mahogany two-day clock with grande-sonnerie striking employing springs for the striking and chiming and a weight for the going train. It dates from *c*1845.
Centre A walnut clock of three-month duration with seconds-beating pendulum; it is signed by Schönberger, *c*1855.
Right A rosewood-veneered eight-day timepiece, possibly originally with a carved cresting on top. Note that all the veneers are laid so that they run vertically.

— **4** —

AUSTRIAN AND GERMAN WALL CLOCKS, 19TH CENTURY

Left A simple eight-day mahogany Vienna timepiece, *c*1835. The clock has canted front corners, a one-piece dial and a steel rod pendulum, always a nice quality feature.
Right An eight-day rosewood grande-sonnerie striking Viennese wall clock, again with carved crested moulding but in this case with a two-piece dial and a pie-crust bezel.
Centre Both the Viennese and Germans made some longcase clocks, although they number only a fraction of the production of wall clocks. Here is a German example with a well-figured walnut case, *c*1880–90. There is a key drawer in the base and a seconds-beating, fully compensated five-rod gridiron pendulum. Most of the grid-iron pendulums seen on later German wall clocks are purely decorative and have no effective compensation.

— **5** —

SECONDS-BEATING GERMAN WALL REGULATOR, LATE 19TH CENTURY

This late-19th-century German 'full-length' walnut wall regulator features a wood rod pendulum and a centre-sweep seconds hand. The movement of the clock strikes on a gong.

Length: 5 ft 4 in (1.6 m).

— **6** —

VIENNESE AND GERMAN WALL REGULATORS, MID TO LATE 19TH CENTURY

Left A miniature single-weighted Viennese wall regulator, *c*1860.

Right A Viennese satin-beech striking wall regulator, *c*1855. Its two-piece dial has a pie-crust bezel.

Centre A typical weight-driven German wall regulator of the 1880s, of the type that was turned out in large numbers by firms such as Lenzkirch and Gustav Becker. Note that by this stage the cases, while often still well constructed, are relatively fussy and lack the simple, elegant lines of the early Viennese clocks. By this time the hands, instead of being pierced out by hand, were usually stamped out by machine.

The years 1800 to 1860 are considered the golden age of Austrian clockmaking. The ingenuity of the clockmakers during that period was, on many occasions, quite exceptional, with clocks being produced with various types of compensated pendulums, complex calendar work and often of long duration (anything up to a year and even more). Throughout this time the number of clockmakers employed continued to increase and it was only with the onset of mass-produced clocks – very similar in general appearance and made in southern Germany from 1870 onward by firms such as Gustav Becker, Junghans, and Lenzkirch – that the Austrian clockmaking industry declined.

Although these later clocks were often of quite good quality, they cannot compare with those made in the Biedermeier period in Vienna. There is a minimum of hand-finishing, for instance, the hands usually stamped out and the dial bezels of simple forms and spun up out of thin brass rather than cast.

As the end of the century approached, cases became far heavier, weighed down by what many would consider excessive ornamentation. At this time spring-driven clocks, sometimes smaller than the standard size, started to appear. No doubt this was in part to decrease the cost of manufacture, an important factor because of the intense competition from American clocks at that time.

— **7** —

BLACK FOREST WALL CLOCKS, 19TH CENTURY

This trio of wall clocks was made in the Black Forest area of Germany in the first half of the 19th century. They all have wooden movements and painted wooden dials and are of 30-hour duration.

The example on the left is a musical clock and has glass bells, while the one in the centre is an automaton clock with a monk tolling the bell at each hour.

— **8** —

MALTESE WALL CLOCK, EARLY 19TH CENTURY

The decorative clock seen here is of a style unique to Malta, where clock cases were nearly always painted. The double front doors are a most unusual feature; both are full-width and sit one behind the other. When opened the first gives access to the hand and winding holes and the second to the movement, which is usually weight-driven, with one weight falling on either side. Occasionally imported movements were employed, as in this instance, where a Viennese grande-sonnerie striking movement of two-day duration has been used.

8

American Shelf and Wall Clocks

Following the War of Independence in America, there was a shortage of materials and a rapidly growing demand for cheaper and smaller clocks than the longcase. Several clockmakers, backed up by the wealth of experience of immigrant clockmakers from such countries as England, The Netherlands and Germany, devised methods of fulfilling this demand by designing and making clock machinery that could be easily produced by factory techniques as opposed to handcrafted production methods. Possibly the most famous of these clockmakers was Eli Terry (1772–1853), who by 1810 had filled an order for some 4,000 clocks. Other makers involved in the early days of factory production were Seth Thomas, Chauncey Jerome and Simon Willard, who made a most attractive banjo clock.

The earlier clocks were usually weight-driven timepieces, but by 1840 striking spring-driven clocks had been introduced. Many distinctive styles evolved during the 19th century, of which the best known group probably comprises shelf clocks. Other distinctive styles are the lighthouse clock by Simon Willard, the lyre clock, the banjo clock, the acorn clock, pillar and scroll clocks, and both steeple and steeple on steeple clocks. A considerable number of novelty clocks were also produced during the century.

One of the most interesting clocks made at this time was the so-called wagon spring. The term wagon spring refers to the way in which the clock is driven, with a large leaf spring at the base of the clock being flexed at either end to give the clock its motive power – and resembling the spring of a wagon. Its invention was brought about because at the time there was no manufacturer of coiled springs in the whole of the United States.

Another fascinating clock, which was first devised in the United States but subsequently gained worldwide popularity, was the torsion clock, invented by Aaron Crane. Its escapement was activated by the very slow winding and unwinding of a steel strip, which only required minimal power and enabled clocks of one-year duration to be made relatively easily. This invention gave rise in Europe to the production of the 400-day or anniversary clock.

— ❶ —

SHELF CLOCK, DAVID WILLIAMS, NEWPORT, RHODE ISLAND

Shelf clocks were among the earliest American clocks to be produced in any quantity and are somewhat similar to shortened longcase clocks. They average 2½–3½ ft (75– 105 cm) in height with an upper structure carrying the clock and dial and a base with a panel, sometimes hinged, that was finished in a variety of ways, for instance, in a wood such as mahogany, with painted decoration or with a mirror.

Such clocks were commonly known as 'Massachusetts shelf clocks', though they were made in several New England states. Other names given to them are 'box on box' or 'case on case' clocks.

Most of the movements are time only, but sometimes they are equipped with an alarm and have a pendulum at the rear.

There are two basic case styles. The first features the so-called kidney dial, with the name of the maker usually below the chapter ring. The door frame and dial surround follow the outline of the dial. The panel in the lower part of the case is usually of wood, with or without inlay. The other style comprises a round convex dial and a glazed door reverse-painted (except where the dial is). Most commonly, the panel in the box is also reverse-painted glass, but it may be mirrored or of wood.

The eight-day weight-driven timepiece shown here, by David Williams, has a solid mahogany case with fan inlay at the corners and a removable flat-topped hood with three brass finials. There is a kidney-shaped painted door and dial. The latter is white-painted metal with floral and gilt decoration.

Height: 39½ in (100 cm).

— ❷ —

PILLAR AND SCROLL CLOCK, ELI TERRY, PLYMOUTH, CONNECTICUT, 1820

This particular style of case, together with its wooden 30-hour movement, was developed by Eli Terry in the wake of his successful completion of the Porter Contract, when he manufactured 4,000 complete clock movements at four dollars each over a period of three years. The development of this type of clock resulted in the rapid growth of the clock-making industry in western Connecticut.

The clock shown here has three solid brass finials and a wooden white-painted dial with black Arabic numerals and floral decoration with gold borders in the

corners. In the lower portion of the door is a reverse painting on glass of Mount Vernon, with an aperture in the centre through which the pendulum bob may be seen. The 30-hour, weight-driven wooden striking movement has a visible escapement. A label on the backboard of the clock reads 'Patent/Invented/Made and Sold by Eli Terry/Plymouth/Conn'. In pencil at the upper right is the date 14 December 1820.

Height: 29 in (73.6 cm).

**GRANDMOTHER OR
'DWARF TALL' CASE CLOCK,
JOSHUA WILDER, HINGHAM,
MASSACHUSETTS, 1820**

These types of clocks are in actuality short longcase clocks. They were not successful, however, in part because, due to their many components, they were not much cheaper to make than a full-sized tall-case clock. Another disadvantage was that they were too short to be placed on the floor and too tall for the shelf. Most of them were made between 1810 and 1830. More clocks by Joshua Wilder (1786–1860) have survived than by any other maker.

The movements are often compact versions of those in tall-case clocks. However, many were just time-only or time and alarm. Some of the cases re-semble scaled-down tall-cases with removable hoods, while others have fixed hoods with access from the rear only.

The Wilder clock seen here has a dark-stained pine case and a fixed hood with brass eagle finial and freestanding columns on either side of the arched door. The brass eight-day weight-driven movement is fitted with an alarm. The white-painted metal dial has Arabic numerals and shield and gilt scroll spandrels in the arch. It is signed 'J. Wilder/Hingham' below the hand arbor and the winding holes have escutcheons inscribed 'Alarm' (left) and 'Time' (right), with arrows to show the direction of winding.

Height: 43 in (109 cm).

— **4** —

BANJO CLOCK, C1815

In 1802 Simon Willard patented the banjo clock, and these have continued to be made, right up until the present day. Some had a simple box at the base, whereas others had decoration coming down below this. Many of the later examples in particular lost the quality and excellent lines of Simon Willard's original design. Probably the finest of the early banjo clocks was the so-called girandole, which was made in small numbers between 1815 and 1818 by Lemuel Curtis.

Among those who made banjo clocks were Aaron Willard, Sawin & Dyer of Boston, the New Haven Clock Company, Seth Thomas and Edward Howard.

The *c*1815 example seen here has a mahogany and gilt-wood case with an 8 in (20 cm) painted dial. The weight-driven timepiece movement has an anchor escapement with the pendulum mounted at the front. The *verre églomisé* (reverse-painted) panel in the base depicts Perry's victory, and there is a similar decoration on the trunk.

— **5** —

**BANJO-SHAPED CLOCK,
HOWARD & DAVIS, BOSTON,
MASSACHUSETTS, 1842–49**

This style of case, although not original to Edward Howard, was used extensively by him for many years. The example seen in the picture here is in a rosewood-simulated case of cherrywood.

The glazing on the trunk and the base is reverse-painted in black and gold with clear glass in the centre. Inscribed on the lower glass in gold letters is 'U.S. Light House Establishment'.

A simple eight-day weight-driven timepiece movement is used.

Height: 32 in (81.2 cm)

— **6** —

**LYRE CLOCK, SAWIN & DYER,
BOSTON, MASSACHUSETTS, C1825**

This is a more ornate form of banjo clock, with applied decoration at the front. It is possible that John Sawin, who was an apprentice of Aaron Willard, may have originated this style in the United States.

The clock has a mahogany and pine case with applied carved gilt decoration. The glass of the trunk is reverse-painted with four vertical pink lines on the blue background to represent the strings. There is an acorn finial on top, and the white-painted dial has a cast brass bezel with convex glass.

The simple weight-driven brass timepiece movement is of eight-day duration.

— **7** —

WAGON SPRING CLOCK WITH FOUR CANDLES, BIRGE & FULLER, BRISTOL, CONNECTICUT, 1845

The powering of clocks by means of a wagon spring was pioneered by Joseph Ives of Bristol around 1825–30 and continued by Birge & Fuller, an example of whose work is seen here. Ives' clocks were of eight-day duration, but others were produced which went for one day or even a month, these being made by Atkins, also of Bristol, from 1850 to 1856. Interestingly, Lagville of Chalons in France made a clock powered by a wagon spring as early as 1680.

A label on the back of the clock shown here reads as follows:

Patent
Accelerating Lever Spring
Eight Day Brass Clocks
Made And For Sale Wholesale And Retail By
Birge & Fuller Bristol, Conn
Warranted If Well Used
Directions For Regulating The Clock

If The Clock Should Run Too Slow,
Raise The Pendulum Ball
By Means Of A Screw At The Bottom and If Too Fast
Lower The Ball In The Same Manner: It Should Be
Taken Off To Do It

The line drawing of this clock, now in The Time Museum in Illinois, explains how the mechanism works. The clock is illustrated with the left-hand train unwound. Applying the key to the winding square **A** the line **B** is drawn up and rotates the barrel **C,** thereby wrapping up the light chain **D**; this in turn draws up the lever **E,** which has an integral tail **F.** Hooked over **F** is a heavy link chain that connects to the outer end of the wagon spring **G.** This spring is firmly fixed at its centre point and, when fully wound, deflects as seen at its right-hand end in the illustration.

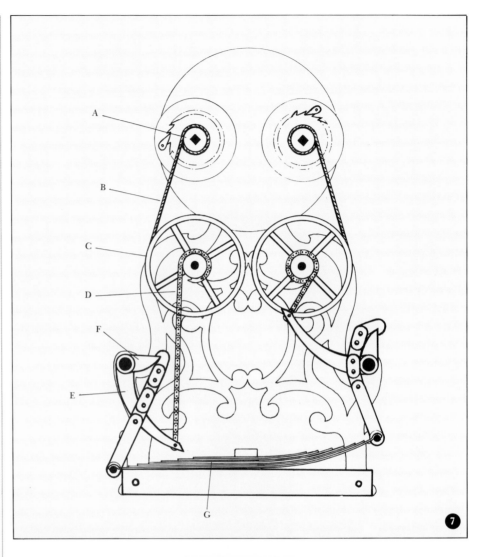

— **8** —

ACORN CLOCK,

FORESTVILLE MFG CO, BRISTOL,

CONNECTICUT, 1835—40

This rare case style was produced by J C Brown's Forestville Clock Co, which was only in business from 1835 to 1840. Brown (1807–72) was involved in several clockmaking partnerships during his lifetime. Always an innovator, he produced many different case styles, such as ripple-front beehives and steeples. The acorn clock was unusual for its time in its use of laminated wood, which was employed to achieve the curved sides of the case and the sidearms. Interestingly, the shape of the movement plates follows the shape of the case.

An unusual feature of the clock is the use of wooden fusees mounted at the bottom of the case, a long way below the movement. At a later date the fusees were incorporated in the movement itself.

The glass panels in the front were decorated with various motifs, including flowers and, as in this particular instance, a building, the Merchants Exchange in Philadelphia.

— 9 —

DOUBLE-DIALLED CALENDAR CLOCK, ITHACA CALENDAR CLOCK CO, ITHACA, NEW YORK, 1865–1914

During the second half of the 19th century, the perpetual calendar clock became an important item in the catalogues of Seth Thomas, E N Welch and other surviving clock companies. Seth Thomas used designs patented by his own engineers (and others), while Welch primarily used the B B Lewis patented design. The Ithaca Calendar Clock Co was formed to manufacture clocks based on H B Horton patents. Ithaca used movements made by Connecticut factories, including E N Welch.

It is believed that the first American calendar operated by clock machinery was patented in 1853 by an Ithaca inventor named J H Hawes, but this calendar was not 'perpetual' since it did not adjust for leap years. It was later improved by another inventor to make this adjustment and placed in the hands of James E and Eugene M Mix, also of Ithaca. The Mix brothers improved on the mechanism and obtained a patent on it in 1860, which was later purchased by the Seth Thomas Clock Company.

In 1865 H B Horton obtained a patent on an improved perpetual calendar mechanism, covering eight claims. Later this design was further improved with nine additional claims. Horton tried to sell his patent to Seth Thomas of Waterbury. The latter offered to buy the patent rights for $300. Horton then persuaded three other Ithaca men to put up $200 each and form a company to manufacture the device. With another $200 from Horton, the new Ithaca Calendar Clock Co started business with $800 capital. The first clocks had iron cases and used purchased movements to conserve capital. The company grew from that base.

The walnut-cased clock shown here has two dials. The upper one has Roman hour numerals and minute and hour hands, and the lower dial is marked 1 to 31 for the days of the month and has apertures to the left and right for the days of the week and the months of the year, respectively. Below 12 o'clock is an aperture displaying the pendulum.

On the dial is written 'Manufactured by The Ithaca Calendar Clock Co Ithaca NY. Patented April 18th 1865 and August 1866'. Inside the case is part of a paper label, dated 1881.

The eight-day spring-driven, gong-striking movement with countwheel is stamped on the front plate 'Manfd for the Ithaca Calendar Clock Co. E. N. Welch Mfg Co'. It has a wire link to the H B Horton patent perpetual calendar mechanism located behind the lower dial.

— **10** —

PORCELAIN SHELF CLOCK,

ANSONIA CLOCK CO,

NEW YORK, C1914

The Ansonia Clock Co was one of the most successful American clock companies. It was founded in Bristol, Connecticut, in 1850 and moved to New York in 1877. At one stage the company was producing over 200 different designs of clock. The porcelain shelf clocks, of which an example is shown here, were made during the first 20 years of this century using American and German cases.

— **11** —

TRIPLE-DECKER SHELF CLOCK,

DYER, WADSWORTH AND

COMPANY, AUGUSTA,

GEORGIA, C1835

As more manufacturers began to produce shelf clocks the competition became fiercer and various decorative features were added to try and achieve sales. Carved designs and fancy tablets became increasingly prominent.

The 'Triple-Decker' or three door shelf clock with carving and gilded columns was an attempt to incorporate all

of the most desirable and expensive features in one clock. It employs a brass 8-day movement made by Birge, Mallory and Co.

— ⑫ —

**REPEATING SHELF CLOCK,
C & N JEROME, BRISTOL,
CONNECTICUT, C1835**

The firm C & N (Chauncey and Noble) Jerome only appears to have operated from 1834 to 1839. They purchased components, including movements, from various suppliers such as Joseph Ives and E C Brewster and Co, who supplied the movement for this repeating shelf clock. It is made of brass and has a duration of 8 days. Although it is called a repeating clock, the strike cannot be repeated at will and thus the term may only refer to the clock's reliability.

— ⑬ —

**SHELF CLOCK,
WELCH MANUFACTURING
COMPANY, FORESTVILLE,
CONNECTICUT, C1880–90**

This very successful manufacturer was active from *c*1850 until 1903, when it became The Sessions Clock Company. The type of clock shown here is typical of the kind of clock they were producing in the 1880s.

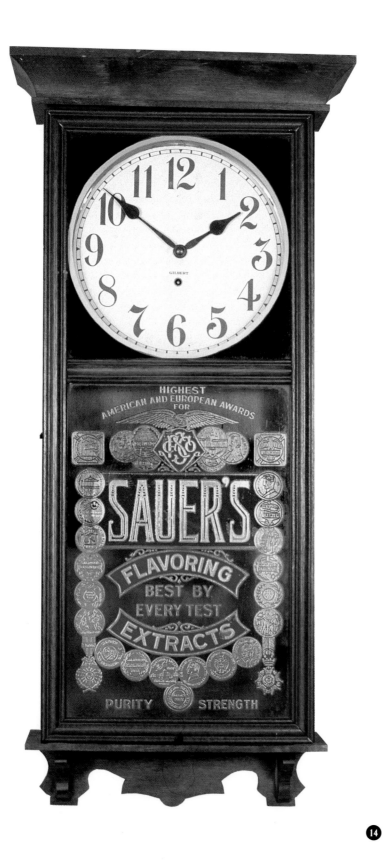

— **14** —

ADVERTISING WALL CLOCK GILBERT CLOCK COMPANY, WINSTED, CONNECTICUT, C1920

William Gilbert founded his very successful clock company in 1825, and the company was to continue in business until it was sold to the Spartus Company of Chicago in 1964.

This eight day timepiece, some 40 in (100 cm) long, has a movement with steel plates incorporating brass bushings. It was manufactured for C F Sauer Co who made flavourings and extracts. The decoration of the front door is achieved by etching, reverse painting and the application of gold leaf.

— **15** —

WALL CLOCK, LITCHFIELD MANUFACTURING COMPANY, LITCHFIELD, CONNECTICUT, C1853

The Litchfield Manufacturing Company made 30-hour timepieces from 1851 to 1854 using movements by Matthews and Jewel of Bristol, Connecticut.

In 1854 P T Barnum, a director of the firm, moved the company to East Bridgeport and joined with Theodore Terry to form the Terry & Barnum Manufacturing Company.

The decorative case of the clock seen here is made out of papier mâché with mother-of-pearl inlay.

14

16

— **16** —

IRON CASED CLOCK, ITHACA CALENDER CLOCK COMPANY, ITHACA, NEW YORK, C1866

Iron clock cases were invented and patented by H B Horton in 1866 and produced by the J S Reynolds foundry in Ithaca for the Ithaca Calender Clock Company in two different styles, the larger one of which is seen here. Although the cases were initially cheaper to make than wooden ones, they only stayed in production for about 10 years.

The perpetual calender also makes use of Horton patents. The timepiece movement made by Laporte Hubbell employs two mainsprings which give a duration of 30 days.

15

Skeleton Clocks

The skeleton clock was devised to display the clockmaker's skill and ingenuity as comprehensively as possible. To that end no case was provided, just a protective glass dome or a glazed brass frame. The dial was frequently fretted out and its centre omitted; the movement plates, particularly on English clocks, also were fretted out.

This design of clock gradually evolved, in the last half of the 18th century, from the fine *pendules de cheminée* being made in France. It was a time of patronage and also great wealth, albeit for a relatively small number of people. They demanded and wanted to be seen to have the best and, happily, this coincided with the greatest period in French horology, with such superb makers as Janvier, Berthoud, Lépine, the Lepautes, Bailly and Breguet, to name but a few, arriving on the scene.

French Skeleton Clocks

· · · · · ·

Up until around 1800 French skeleton clocks all tended to be different, and they were often very complex, employing for instance, a *remontoir*, most commonly a device for converting a spring-driven clock into a weight-driven one by using the mainspring to wind up a small weight at regular, generally short, intervals. This provides much more even power than a spring and thus improves the timekeeping.

Other additional features added to the clock at this time included the moon's age and phases, simple and perpetual calendar work, and an additional hand, so that both mean (our time) and solar time are shown and thus also the 'equation of time', that is, the difference between our time and that shown on a sundial.

After 1800–10, although fascinating one-off clocks continued to be produced, certain standardized designs were also made, though in very small numbers. Examples of these are the beautiful glass-plated clocks, possibly the ultimate in skeleton-clock design, which often go for six months on one winding. A similar but keyhole-framed design was also produced, and Verneuil made a series of fine and often quite large calendar skeleton clocks.

One of the best known French skeleton clocks was that shown at the Great Exhibition in London in 1851. A most attractive piece only around 10 in (25.4 cm) tall, it was produced over a long period in appreciable numbers and in several different forms.

— ❶ —

FRENCH SKELETON CLOCK, VERNEUIL, LATE 18TH CENTURY

This spectacular clock is signed by Verneuil. Showing strong Egyptian and Roman influence, its design was stimulated no doubt by Napoleon's famous victories around that time (it was photographed at Schoonhoven in The Netherlands by courtesy of museum authorities there). The two-train movement has a pinwheel escapement and a beautifully executed nine-rod gridiron pendulum with beat regulation.

The lunar dial at the top is one of the finest the author has seen on a clock. A lake with a boat and a castle are shown in the foreground and an erupting volcano behind. Pearls are set in at the bottom of each side of the lunar calendar. The dials at the bottom left give the days of the week, their deities and the months of the year, and on the right are shown the days of the month and the signs of the zodiac.

Height: 30½ in (76.2 cm)

— ❷ —

FRENCH GLASS-PLATED
SKELETON CLOCK, C1800

The French glass-plated skeleton clocks made around 1800 – in which all the wheelwork is apparently suspended in midair, there being no visible frame – are undoubtedly the ultimate in skeleton-clock design and execution and are always a joy to behold.

This particular example, which is of six-month duration, has such delicate wheelwork that one wonders how it has survived for so long in such excellent condition. The thinnest wheel is only 0.016 in (0.4 mm) thick. The great wheel, a little over 9 in (23 cm) in diameter has five Y-shaped spokes and the others four or five tapering spokes. The very delicate pinwheel escapement is controlled by a steel rod pendulum with brass bob, which has knife-edge suspension and is provided with beat regulation.

The strike is powered by a small *remontoir* spring, which is rewound from the large spring barrel mounted at the centre of the great wheel. The strike is regulated by a large countwheel, with a bell fixed below the glass plate being struck by a hammer mounted at the end of a long vertical arbor. The fly is three-bladed. The enamelled chapter ring, which is dished and very fully cut out in the centre, has decorative Arabic hour and Roman minute numerals with fine engine-turned inner and outer fire-gilt bezels. The glass plate is supported by two gilded scrolls that rest on a white marble base.

Height: 22½ in (57 cm)

Train Count		
	Teeth	Pinion Leaves
Great Wheel	400	
Centre Wheel	248	12
Third Wheel	300	10
'Scape Wheel	60	6
Strike Countwheel	400	12
Strike	200	6
Fly		6

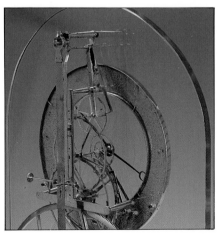

3

These attractive little clocks, commonly known as Great Exhibition skeleton clocks, were designed and produced by Victor Pierret of Paris from the 1840s to the end of the century and appeared in a variety of forms. For instance, they were available with and without engraving and they might have an alarm concealed within the base and wound by a cord coming out of one side. A second cord on the other side was provided to set the time at which the alarm went off by rotating the alarm disc in the centre of the dial. The example shown here is with engraving but without alarm.

The clocks are so called because they were exhibited and sold in relatively large numbers at the Great Exhibition in London in 1851.

4

VIENNESE SKELETON CLOCK,
C 1820—30

This most attractive Viennese skeleton clock, *c*1820–30, is of eight-day duration and has a fine driving weight decorated with engine turning.

The clock features an engraved and silvered brass chapter ring with inner and outer engine-turned bezels. Through the centre the delicately skeletonized movement may be seen. There is beautifully shaped knife-edge suspension to the pendulum, which has a glazed bob, in the centre of which are displayed the pivoted levers for Ellicott's form of compensation.

The movement is supported by two Bohemian cut-glass columns with red overlay and ormolu mounts.

Height: 22½ in (57.2 cm)

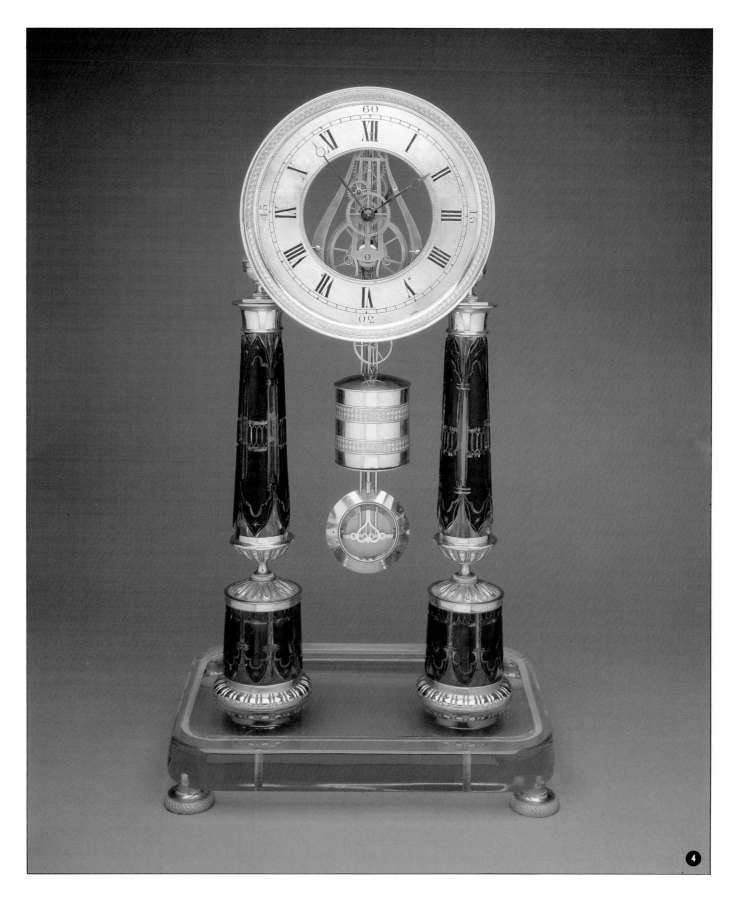

Austrian Skeleton Clocks
· · · · · · ·

The manufacture of skeleton clocks in the Austro-Hungarian Empire was mainly concentrated in Vienna and commenced around 1800. Although these Austrian models were quite often strongly influenced by French clocks, they rapidly assumed their own individuality. Many of the earlier examples were of considerable complexity and ingenuity – for instance, quite a few were weight-driven – but the later pieces tended to be fairly standardized, usually spring-driven, of two-day duration and having quarter-striking. They were also far more ornate.

English Skeleton Clocks
· · · · · · ·

Skeleton-clock manufacture started in England around 1820, the earlier examples copying the basic French styles and usually employing an inverted Y-shaped frame. Relatively few skeleton clocks were made prior to 1835, but after this time production escalated rapidly, no doubt strongly influenced by the increasing momentum of the Industrial Revolution. Indeed, by 1850–60 the numbers being made vastly exceeded those that had been produced in France and Austria.

One of the first of what might be termed the purely English designs was the simple Gothic frame, usually only 11–12 in (28–30.5 cm) tall and generally just a timepiece. This was quickly followed by the scroll frame, Edwards of Stourbridge being one of its first producers.

There was a rapid increase in the range of clocks available. Even musical clocks were now being offered, and the variety of frames was greatly extended. Many were based on famous buildings, such as Lichfield Cathedral, York Minster and Brighton Pavilion. Floral designs were also produced, incorporating, for instance, fuchsias and ivy leaves.

The vast majority of skeleton clocks were produced by a few specialist manufacturers, such as Evans of Handsworth (Birmingham) and Smith of Clerkenwell (London), but there were also other clock-makers who, although they made relatively small numbers of skeleton clocks, produced some superb quality and highly ingenious pieces. Examples that spring to mind are James Condliff's beautifully proportioned and excellently made clocks, which quite frequently employ a seconds-beating balance. Pace also made some fascinating clocks.

By 1890 the heyday of the English skeleton clock was over and 20 years later only a few simple timepieces were being produced.

— **5** —

AUSTRIAN SKELETON CLOCK, MID 19TH CENTURY

This Austrian skeleton clock epitomizes the gaiety and fun of Vienna at mid-century, with its ornate wood frame decorated with gold leaf and smothered with silver repoussé work. The silver of the base incorporates figures, a cornucopia of flowers and floral swags. There is silver floral strapwork curling up the pillars and behind the pendulum, the bob of which is fretted out and decorated with coloured stones; behind it is a harp.

The silvered-brass dial has Roman numerals and a fretted-out brass centre. The ornate silvered bezel incorporates a cherub. The 30-hour movement strikes the halves and hours on a gong, and there is a music box in the base of the clock that plays one of two tunes sequentially, either on the hour or when the repeat cord is pulled.

Height: 22 in (55.8 cm)

— **6** —

ENGLISH SKELETON CLOCK, C1825

A typical example of an early English skeleton clock, this model features the inverted Y-frame, which was so popular with French makers and was also being used in England at this time. It has a large great wheel with fusee. Although unsigned, it is probably reasonable to attribute this clock to the maker White-hurst of Derby.

The frame is far more substantial than that on an equivalent French clock and is beautifully finished. The wheelwork has five crossings and rests on turned and knurled brass feet. The great wheel is some 4½ in (11.4 cm) in diameter; dead-beat escapement is provided, and there is a gilded chapter ring with Roman numerals that is attractively bevelled on its inner and outer edges.

The wood rod pendulum is a particularly attractive feature of the clock, with regulation above the well-turned bob The clock rests on a straight-sided black marble base with ormolu mounts, and has a rectangular glazed cover with delicate brass frame.

Height: 15 in (38 cm)

— 7 —

ENGLISH GOTHIC-FRAME
SKELETON CLOCK, C1840

The simple Gothic frame followed fairly close on the heel of the inverted Y-frame and was mainly used between 1835 and 1850, after which time it tended to be replaced by the architectural clocks.

This *c*1840 example has stepped frames no less than ½ in (1.3 cm) thick that are surmounted by crosses. Six attractively turned pillars are employed with decorative screwed collets at either end. There is a going barrel with a 4 in (10 cm) great wheel. The wheelwork has either five or six delicate crossings, and a dead-beat escapement is used. The pendulum matches up to the quality of the rest of the clock, the regulating nut being contained in a cage above the bob.

The clock has brass ball feet that rest on a velvet-covered rosewood base.

Height: 15 in (38 cm)

— 8 —

ENGLISH SKELETON CLOCK,
W WILSON, MARYPORT, C1869–70

A highly ingenious eight-day skeleton clock of considerable complexity, this was made by W Wilson of Maryport, who is recorded as making clocks from 1869 to 1870.

The clock has four spring barrels and four fusees, the outer two being for the going and striking train, with fusees mounted high up in the frame and the inner pair with fusees situated at the bottom above the Swiss musical movement, which it powers via a drive shaft and a series of bevel gears.

The times at which the music is played are both practical and highly individual. It plays automatically every two hours from a selection of six tunes between the hours of 10 AM and 8 PM inclusive and is silent at night, thus both conserving power and avoiding disturbing its owners' sleep. On Sundays, like all good religious clocks, it stays silent. There is also music/silent regulation and provision to play the same tune continuously or to change each time.

The movement has a pin-pallet lever escapement with a blued-steel spiral hairspring, is fitted with maintaining power, and in addition to the main dial, has additional dials – all attractively engraved for the days of the week, days of the month and months of the year. The calendar work is annual-perpetual, which means that it allows for the short months of the year.

The clock rests on a beautiful floral-carved mahogany base with gilt decoration and has carved feet.

Height: 22 in (55.8 cm)

— 9 —

ENGLISH SKELETON CLOCK BASED ON YORK MINSTER, ATTRIBUTED TO SMITH OF CLERKENWELL, MID 19TH CENTURY

By around 1845 skeleton clocks based on famous buildings started to appear. The first of those copied was the Scott Memorial, which recently had been completed in Edinburgh. This was produced by Evans of Handsworth (Birmingham) and sold in large numbers throughout Scotland. Other buildings copied included York Minster, Westminster Abbey, Lichfield Cathedral and the Brighton Pavilion.

The example pictured is the only skeleton clock the author has encountered based on York Minster Cathedral that may be safely attributed to Smith of Clerkenwell. All the others known have been made by Evans and, while invariably of good quality, lack the delicacy and attention to detail of this piece.

The clock would have been made for exhibition purposes or for a special presentation, judging by the beautifully executed plaque on the front. Everything is pierced out extremely finely to the highest of standards.

The base, frames, cover and chapter ring, which is one of the finest the author has seen, are all decorated with engraving; the snail and star wheel are carefully skeletonized, and the wheelwork is five-spoke.

The clock rests on a substantial gilded three-tier plinth and still has its original base and dome. It is signed by Hamilton and Co, London and Calcutta, who were its distributors.

Overall height: 21½ in (54.6 cm)

— ⑩ —

GROUP OF ENGLISH SKELETON CLOCKS, MID 19TH CENTURY

TOP ROW

Left This highly individual single-train skeleton train clock is attractively signed on the base, 'J. Pace, Bury St Edmunds'. The very heavy plates with chamfered edges rest on a substantial oval brass base. The gilded dial is fully fretted out. Mounted above this is the going barrel with a train of delicate six-spoke wheels running up vertically to the five-spoke 'scape wheel, which is dead-beat. At the top of the frame is the regulation for fast/slow. A most unusual feature is the mounting of a pulley on the backplate at the rear of the centre wheel arbor, from which a cord runs down to drive the minute arbor. It has a hatchet-shaped pendulum bob.

A similar clock was described in the 1851 Great Exhibition catalogue.

Centre This pretty little French Great Exhibition skeleton timepiece, with silk suspension, anchor escapement and enamelled dial, is signed 'Hatton Paris'. It is without an alarm, and the frame is not engraved. It is also signed on the brass baseplate, 'Ms Honorables, Paris'.

Height: 8¾ in (22.2 cm)

Right This English mid-19th-century twin fusee scroll-frame skeleton clock strikes on a bell mounted above the movement. There are six attractively turned pillars; the snail is skeletonized and has an engraved and silvered brass chapter ring with scalloped border. The clock is complete with well-fitting glass dome and brass-inlaid rosewood base. It was made by Evans of Handsworth.

BOTTOM ROW

Left This substantial twin-chain fusee skeleton clock, c1860, features a passing half-hour and full-hour strike on a bell. The frame, which employs six pillars, is attractively decorated with ivy leaves, and the silvered-brass chapter ring is well fretted out. The clock rests on four ornamental turned brass feet.

Height: 19 in (48.3 cm)

Centre This is a very rare and lovely little great wheel skeleton timepiece with a short fusee, maintaining power and a large jewelled lever escapement with a balance controlled by a helical hairspring mounted above. It has a silvered chapter ring with fine inner and outer engine-turned bezels and rests on a circular turned brass base into which the spring barrel is partially recessed. The frame pillars are most attractively turned and are held in place by well-finished knurled bolts. The clock rests on a velvet base and has a protection dome. It was made in Liverpool, c1845.

Right This fine-quality single-train fusee skeleton clock with floral frame is almost certainly by Evans of Handsworth, the frame and substantial chapter ring with shield-shaped plaques for the numerals being typical of his work. The wheelwork has six crossings and mounted at the top of the frame is a large and attractively shaped platform carrying the lever escapement; this has a two-tooth escapement wheel above which is the split bi-metallic half-seconds-beating chronometer balance, which has a helical hairspring and is provided with a large seconds ring at the top of the dial.

This is the only skeleton clock the author has seen with this form of escapement.

— ⓫ —

ENGLISH SKELETON CLOCK, JAMES CONDLIFF, C1840

James Condliff was undoubtedly one of the finest – if not *the* finest – English skeleton clockmakers, and this is a typical example of his earlier work.

It has a carved and inlaid mahogany base and numerous decorative mounts, mostly in a classical vein, with simple cupids around the arch, an elephant and stag resting just below the chapter ring, sphinxes (a popular feature in Regency and early Victorian times) on either side of the large balance, with a lion in front of the left-hand barrel. To the right of the balance are two racehorses, which probably relate to the commencement of the Grand National in Liverpool in 1839. The feet on which the base rests have a Regency look. Although no presentation plaque is present, it is likely that this clock was made for a specific person and may well have been designed to reflect his various interests.

The two-train movement has pump-action quarter chime on two gongs mounted in the base, and the skeletonized snail in the centre of the dial that controls this is very much a decorative feature of the clock. The fine wheelwork has six crossings, and maintaining power is provided and can be seen quite clearly in a rear view of the clock. The enamelled chapter ring has an engine-turned outer and smooth inner bezel. An additional wheel has been provided in the striking train, situated to the left of the clock, which is presumably to allow for the additional power required for the quarter-striking, but also has the added advantage of producing symmetry in the line of the two chains.

Mystery, Novelty and Fantasy Clocks

A s their names imply, these clocks are designed not just to tell the time, but to fascinate in one way or another, for instance, by mystifying you as to how they work or amusing you with the way in which they do so, maybe with automata (moving figures) that perform either when the clock is going or when it strikes.

The first of these clocks originated in southern Germany in the 17th century. Clocks were produced in the forms of animals and people whose eyes moved in time with the pendulum. Others were far more complex, for example, the arms, legs, neck or head might move, imitating an action such as eating. One of the most fascinating is the Chariot Clock in The Time Museum, Rockford, Illinois, which shows the gluttonous mythical King Gambrinus sitting on a chariot. As the vehicle gradually proceeds down the dining table under its own power, the monarch raises a tankard in his right hand to his mouth, which opens and closes as he does so.

In the 19th century the French produced a series of clocks designed to mystify everyone regarding how they worked. There is no apparent movement behind the dial, for example, or the hands, mounted on a glass dial, appear to have no possible means of driving them, or the movement situated in the base is separated from the dial by a glass column and thus has no visible means of connection. Many of these clocks were made by the brilliant illusionist Robert Houdin *c*1840–60. Some fine automata were also made, such as tightrope walkers and jugglers. Another fascinating clock produced around this time indicated the hours and minutes by means of a girl's arms rising and falling.

The blinking-eye clocks, which originated in Augsburg in the 17th century, were produced in simplified form in southern Germany in the mid 19th century and also in the United States. The latter were nearly all made of cast iron in the form of minstrels, dogs or lions.

A further ingenious series of clocks was made in France from around 1880 to 1910. These were mostly associated with the Industrial Revolution and showed, for instance, a steam hammer or a beam engine at work, or a lighthouse revolving.

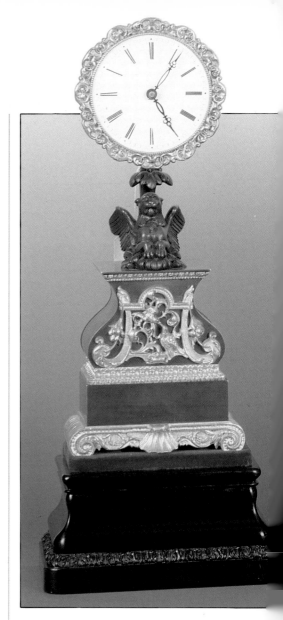

— ❶ —

FRENCH MYSTERY CLOCK, C1850

This is an example of a fascinating and beautifully executed French mystery clock, in which the dial has no apparent connection with the movement.

The clock, which rests on a velvet-covered ebonized base, is of bronze with fine gilt mounts with eagles depicted in the centre. Sitting on a plate above the main body of the clock is a winged griffin and rising up behind is scrolling foliage that contains the drive to the dial. The two-train movement, which strikes on a bell, is housed within the main body of the clock.

Height: 16½ in (42 cm)

FRENCH MYSTERY CLOCK, C1865

The time on this rare French mystery clock is indicated by the rising and falling arms of a young girl. The finger of her left hand gives the minutes by gradually rising and as it does so it points to a cream enamelled sector divided into five-minute divisions. When it reaches 60, the hand drops back to the bottom of the scale. Her right hand performs a similar function for the hours.

The gilded figure rests against a green and gilt enamelled background and is flanked by gilded pillars. The marble base has decorative ormolu mounts.

Height: 16½ in (42 cm)

GLASS-DIALLED MYSTERY CLOCK, ROBERT HOUDIN, C1845

The brilliant illusionist Robert Houdin created this fascinating glass-dialled mystery clock around 1845. It has a bronze case with gilt-metal mounts and a gold leaf and gesso wooden base.

The mystery is created by having two glass dials, one with the numerals and a second onto which the hour hand is attached. A brass-toothed wheel fixed to the edge of this and concealed by the bezel is driven by bevel gears running up through one of the supports.

Height: 16 in (40.6 cm)

④

5

FRENCH AND AMERICAN
SWINGING CLOCKS,
C 1880—90

These fascinating clocks, popularly known as 'swingers', were produced in a wide variety of sizes in both France and the United States. The smallest examples often incorporated animals and made use of watch movements.

In effect the whole clock is a pendulum, the movement being contained within the sphere at the top, with a smaller lead-filled sphere at the bottom balancing it.
Left An American 'swinger' made by the Ansonia Clock Company, *c*1890.
Height: 25½ in (65 cm)

④

FRENCH MYSTERY CLOCK,
C 1870

A good French mystery clock is seen here, with a Belgian black slate case. Engraved and decorated with giltwork, it rests on ornate gilt-brass feet with ringed carrying handles on either side. It is surmounted by a gilt spelter figure of a girl holding in her outstretched hand the pendulum with glass bob (which has no apparent connection with the movement, as the figure merely rests on the platform and can be lifted off it).

In actual fact, the figure rocks from side to side an imperceptible amount in time with the pendulum, and this motion is transmitted via the platform on which the figure rests to the movement.

Centre A large and particularly attractive 'swinger' with winged Vengeance holding the double-sphere pendulum. The figure is standing next to a bust of a satyr on a Corinthian column; both figures are particularly well modelled and rest on a base with a mahogany pediment. The *c*1880–90 clock is comparatively rare in that it has a striking train. The movement is signed 'Mougin deux Medailles' and numbered 3789.

Height: 41 in (104 cm)

Right An attractive French bronze clock, *c*1880, with the figure of Cupid holding the pendulum.

Height: 35 in (89 cm)

— 6 —

FRENCH STEAM HAMMER CLOCK, C1870–1910

During the period 1870 to 1910 a considerable number of French clocks were made that symbolized aspects of the Industrial Revolution. They were nearly always of fine quality. A typical example of these pieces is the steam hammer clock seen here, which is a close copy of an actual steam hammer. By means of a complex series of linkages and an X-suspension, the hammer – which goes up and down as if to strike the work on the anvil – acts as the pendulum.

Height: 18 in (46 cm)

AMERICAN ASTRONOMICAL YEAR-DURATION TORSION PENDULUM TIMEPIECE, A D CRANE, MID 19TH CENTURY

Aaron D Crane, born in 1804, was an ingenious and self-taught clockmaker, working mainly in Newark, New Jersey. His main claim to fame was the invention of the torsion pendulum, which made possible the mass production of year-duration clocks in the hundreds of thousands, if not millions. Indeed, such clocks are still being made today (they are popularly known as anniversary and 400-day clocks).

The spring-driven clock illustrated here is one of Crane's masterpieces. It is signed in the centre of the lower dial: 'Boston Clock Company. A. D. Crane Patent 375 days Patented Feb 10th 1841. Extended Dec 15th 1851. Improved June 22nd 1852 and Jan 9th 1855.'

The indications given by the astronomical work are: year calendar (not visible here), with signs of the zodiac on a silver ring; times of sunrise/sunset; the passage of the sun through the heavens, and the passage of the moon and the lunar phases.

— 8 —

**TORSIONAL PENDULUM CLOCK,
SILAS B TERRY, ANSONIA/
TERRYVILLE, CONNECTICUT,
MID 19TH CENTURY**

Silas B Terry, one of Eli Terry's sons, was an inventive person who made clocks with interesting movements. Illustrated here is a typical example of the younger Terry's ingenuity, incorporating as it does the early use of the torsion pendulum, which was invented by Aaron Crane.

The clock is signed in a narrow ring inside the chapter ring: 'Ansonia Clock Co. Ansonia CT USA'. The spring barrel pinned to the rear plate is stamped on the backplate: 'Terryville Manufacturing, Terryville, Conn, patented Oct 5th 1852.'

Height: 7½ in (19 cm)

— 9 —

**ROTARY PENDULUM CLOCK,
E N WELCH, BRISTOL,
CONNECTICUT, 1880**

This E N Welch Model II rotary pendulum clock is mounted on a round black wooden base and has a round paper dial. The 30-hour time-only movement has round horizontal plates and a mainspring that is mounted in the base below the movement. The six-spoke winding key is situated underneath this.

The spherical pendulum bob is suspended on a thread from a bracket that extends from the back of the movement. There is a regulating knob on the bracket behind the suspension point. An extension at the bottom of the pendulum engages a wire fixed to the top end of the final arbor of the time train that protrudes through the top plate, thus causing the pendulum to rotate in a conical projection. A red plush collar around the movement protects it from dirt.

Height: 5⅜ in (13.5 cm)

— 10 —

ILLUMINATED ALARM NOVELTY CLOCK, ANSONIA BRASS AND COPPER CO, CONNECTICUT, LATE 19TH CENTURY

Such highly ingenious clocks are similar, in their main action at least, to certain clocks being produced in Germany in the 17th and early 18th centuries. The Connecticut-made example illustrated is basically an alarm clock made by Ansonia Brass and Copper Co in a cottage clock case with an H J Davies lighting mechanism mounted on top. The whole assembly is known as an illuminated alarm clock. When the alarm mechanism is tripped, a lever releases a spring-mounted friction surface against a pre-positioned match, to light it; the match then swings into position to light a kerosene lamp. The patent for this, No 186317, was granted on 16 Jan 1877.

Height: 16 in (40.6 cm)

— 11 —

JOHN BULL BLINKING-EYE CLOCK, BRADLEY AND HUBBARD MANUFACTURING CO, CONNECTICUT, C1860

This clock, which is also known as 'The Squire', was made by Bradley and Hubbard of West Meriden, Connecticut. It has a spring-driven time-only movement by C Jerome.

— 12 —

BLINKING-EYE SHELF CLOCK, C1870

Blinking or moving eyes were a popular feature of several different American clock designs. The example seen here is believed to have been based on one of the characters from Lewis Carroll's *Alice in Wonderland*, which was published in 1865. The Terry Clock Co are thought to have been the manufacturers.

Carriage Clocks

The travelling clock became a far more practical proposition following the invention *c*1500 of the coiled spring to power clocks. Although portable weight-driven clocks were made, these were difficult to use, because a special box was required to keep the clock and weights together: each time it was moved, it had to be packed up and reset in its new location by hanging it on the wall and adding the weights. None of these problems existed with a spring-driven clock.

The most easily portable timekeeper is, of course, the watch, but this is for personal and not general use in the household. Probably the earliest travelling clocks were those made in southern Germany, such as the rectangular or hexagonal table clocks, which often originally had travelling cases. Similar clocks were also made in France and Italy.

French Carriage Clocks

Another form of travelling clock was the coach watch, which was in fact very similar to a giant watch, and in England small bracket clocks were made with travelling cases. However, it was in France that the major developments in travelling clocks took place.

Apart from the clock termed *pendule de voyage,* two distinct styles evolved, one the *pendule d'officier,* the other the *Capucine.* Neither of these, however, had a particularly long life, and they were swept from the scene by the carriage clock.

The first carriage clocks were undoubtedly made by Abraham Louis Breguet, but only in very small numbers; they were both very expensive and usually complex. Although the basic design of these was conceived in Breguet's lifetime, they went on being produced long after his death. In fact, many of the later pieces made in the last part of the 19th century and the beginning of the 20th century were 'bought in' pieces to which Breguet merely added its name and retailed them.

Paul Garnier (1801–69) was the first to produce carriage clocks in any quantity and usually employed his own form of escapement, the chaffcutter. By the late 1830s he had been joined by other makers such as Bolviller, Auguste, Jules, Berolla and Lépine, and by the 1850s carriage clock production was in full swing, with all the benefits that mass production can bring.

❶

— ❶ —

**SWISS PENDULE D'OFFICIER,
ROBERT & COURVOISIER,
GENEVA, C1790**

This style of travelling clock arose in France and the French/Swiss borders in the last quarter of the 18th century and went out of fashion with the advent of the carriage clock some 40 years later.

The finely chased and gilded case has a carrying handle on top and rests on bun feet. The two-train movement has a chain fusee for the time train and a going barrel for the grande-sonnerie striking and repeating, with a lever in the side of the case for grande sonnerie/petite sonnerie/silence. The clock has a pull wind for the alarm. The verge escapement has a vertical balance mounted on the back-plate, and the rack for the strike is also placed externally, a common feature of clocks made in this region at that time.

Height: 8¼ in (21 cm)

— **2** —

FRENCH BREGUET CARRIAGE CLOCK, NO 5017, SOLD 1853

This clock has an enamelled dial with delicate Roman numerals for the hours and Arabics for the remainder. It is signed on the dial 'Breguet' and on the engraved and gilded mask 'Breguet No 5017'.

There are centre-sweep minute and hour hands; seconds below 12 o'clock, days of the month to the left and alarm ring to the right of the dial. To the top left of the dial is regulation for quarters only or hours and quarters and on the top right strike/silent.

There is a repeat button on top, as well as a cord for winding the alarm. It has a lever escapement with three-arm balance and parachute suspension. It is shown complete with its original carrying box, key and certificate, as issued by Breguet (the latter indicates that on 8 June 1853 the clock was sold to Vladimir Komer for 4,000 francs). As with all Breguet's products, each of his carriage clocks, although basically similar, has many individual features.

All the clocks in this series were designed by Abraham Louis Breguet and started to be made during his life, but were completed over a longer period.

2

— **3** —

FRENCH GARNIER CARRIAGE CLOCK, NO 3697, 1845

This is a finely engraved but comparatively late example of the work of Paul Garnier. It still retains the overall proportions of his earlier clocks, though these usually had front wind through an engine-turned silvered dial and a lift-up front door.

3

— **4** —

FRENCH MULTIPIECE CARRIAGE CLOCK, C1835

A relatively early French carriage clock is seen here, its two-train movement striking and repeating on a gong. A solid back door incorporates shutters for the winding and handset squares and slides for the fast/slow regulation and strike/silent. The well laid out enamelled dial has delicate Roman numerals and subsidiary dials surrounded by gold rings for the alarm and 31-day calendar. It is fitted with a lever escapement with plain

4

balance and has a most attractive carrying handle on top.

The signature on the sides of the plates reads 'Blondeau, Paris', a well-known early maker, examples of whose work are rare. He exhibited in Paris in 1827, 1834 and 1837.

The original carrying case seen in the background is in the early style, with brass latches at the sides and a carrying handle on top. By c1860 a somewhat simpler design of case was being used with a leather strap on top.

Height: 7 in (17.8 cm)

— **5** —

FRENCH GORGE-CASED

CARRIAGE CLOCK, 1880 ᶜ

The gorge case, with its attractive moulds and fluting at the front four corners, was one of the finest and certainly the most popular case style to evolve *c*1860.

The example seen here is what might be termed a full-sized *gorge*-cased carriage clock. It has grande-sonnerie striking on two gongs with a selection lever in the base for striking (hours only)/silent or full striking (hours and quarters at each quarter). The clock is also provided with an alarm and has a solid shuttered back door with the functions of each winding square engraved around the periphery. It is numbered 11115.

Height: 6¾ in (17 cm)

Case Styles

Many different styles of clock case evolved, mostly during the second half of the 19th century. Here we see a few examples. All of the heights are quoted without the handle.

TOP ROW

Left and Centre A miniature (2½ in/ 6.4 cm) and a full-sized (4⅞ in/11.3 cm) *corniche*-cased carriage clock; *c*1880–90.

Right *Doucine* (serpentine-fronted) miniature carriage clock (3 in/7.6 cm) decorated with bands of champlevé enamel at the top and bottom. The circular enamelled dial, with Roman numerals, is surrounded by a gilt mask; *c*1900–10.

BOTTOM ROW

Left A *cannelée*-cased (a simplified form of *gorge*), fully engraved carriage clock (5¼ in/13.3 cm) with strike, repeat and alarm; *c*1880.

Centre A giant *gorge*-cased carriage clock (8½ in/21.6 cm) with strike/repeat and alarm; *c*1875.

Right A fine fully engraved and gilded multipiece striking carriage clock, *c*1840, with a circular enamelled dial that is surrounded by a well-engraved gilt mask (5½ in/14 cm).

Case Sizes

Here the extreme range of sizes of carriage clocks can be seen.

Left A giant (some 10½ in/27 cm high) English fully engraved carriage clock manufactured by the eminent clockmaker James McCabe; *c*1845.
Centre Left A beautiful full-sized porcelain-panelled and engraved *corniche*-cased French carriage clock.
Centre Right A French miniature (2⅞ in/6.2 cm) engraved porcelain-panelled carriage clock.
Right A subminiature (1⅞ in/3.7 cm) Swiss carriage clock with finely executed enamelled panels.

6

— **6** —

ENGLISH ENGRAVED CARRIAGE
CLOCK, C1850

A superbly cast, chased and engraved carriage clock case much in the style of Thomas Cole, with highly decorative columns at the four corners, engraved side panels incorporating heraldic beasts and on the back a basket of flowers. There is an engraved mask surrounding the circular silvered dial. The clock contains an English timepiece movement with a lever escapement and plain balance.

Height: 7 in (18 cm)

7

— **7** —

FRENCH, PORCELAIN-PANELLED,
GORGE-CASED CARRIAGE CLOCK,
DROCOURT, 1880

By about 1860 it became fashionable to decorate carriage clocks with fine panels, often incorporating semiprecious stones. However, these were produced in small numbers as they were expensive to make.

Illustrated is a fine *gorge*-cased carriage clock by Drocourt – numbered 9107 on the backplate, the base and the panels – which strikes and repeats at will on a gong. It has five beautifully executed Sèvres porcelain panels, all with blue grounds and decorated with beads of semiprecious stones and pearls.

The dial has Roman numerals surrounded by a gilt line and with stones between, and the centre has delicately executed swags of flowers. It is signed by E W Streeter, London, the distributor. The four other panels depict country scenes with cottages, ruins, trees, flowers and a lake.

Height: 7 in (18 cm)

As the century went on, the market tended to expand. Some of the best-known makers were: Drocourt, Couaillet, Dumas, Duverdrey & Bloquel, Jacot, Japy Frères, Lamaille, Henry Marc, Margaine, Maurice, Pons, Richard & Cie and Soldano. However, it is difficult to know in what quantities they made the clocks, particularly as the majority are unsigned (probably because most retailers preferred to have just their own name on the dial).

Many different case styles evolved, of which some of the most common are seen in this chapter. Sizes also varied enormously. Although the majority were between 4½ in (11.4 cm) and 6½ in (16.5 cm) high, excluding the handle, miniatures only a little over 2 in (5 cm) were produced, as well as giants going up to 10 in (25.4 cm).

Various types of decoration were introduced to make the carriage clock more appealing, the most common being engraving, which varied greatly in extent and quality. Other ways of decorating clocks included substituting glass panels and plain white dials with decorative porcelain panels, often having a romantic theme. Another popular form of ornamentation was champlevé enamelling. Enamelled panels, usually Limoges, were also used, as were those decorated with multicoloured gold and silver.

Carriage clock production continued at a relatively high level until the outbreak of the First World War in 1914. Although production started again after 1918, far fewer clocks were produced and their output continued to decrease until by 1939 it was very small. They have never stopped being made, however, and probably more carriage clocks are being produced now than in the past 30 to 40 years. Several firms are involved, including some in England. Interestingly, L'Epée in Sainte-Suzanne – which made carriage clocks over a century ago – is still doing so today.

English Carriage Clocks

Although carriage clocks started to be made in England at roughly the same time as they did in France, no serious attempt was made to compete with the French carriage clock industry. The clocks made in England were usually far larger, heavier and much more expensive to manufacture; many still employed chain fusees. Indeed, the exact reverse of the French approach seems to have been adopted, the clocks often apparently having been made regardless of expense and incor-

— **8** —

FRENCH, CHAMPLEVÉ-
ENAMELLED CARRIAGE CLOCK,
C1890

A popular form of decoration applied to metalwork in France in the last half of the 19th century was multicoloured champlevé enamelling, a process in which lacunae (recesses) are cut in brass and then filled with different colours of enamel that are fired individually in a furnace at relatively high temperatures.

Seen here is an exceptionally fine champlevé carriage clock decorated pre-dominantly in blues, pinks, yellows and browns on the handle, the top of the case, the pillars and the base. There are beautifully executed floral gilt frets on either side that are protected by slightly convex glasses, and there is a similar fret around the dial. This is silvered and has recessed plaques for the black Arabic numerals. There is additional gilt fretwork in the centre of the dial. This is signed 'Hall and Co Paris', and the movement is by Maurice (E M & Co), famous for its fine enamelled clocks. The gong striking movement is numbered 4761.

Height: 7½ in (19 cm)

⑨

— ⑨ —

FRENCH, MULTICOLOURED-METAL CARRIAGE CLOCK, LATE 19TH CENTURY

One of the most beautiful finishes to be applied to a carriage clock was that of combined multicoloured golds and silver, which were let into the metal of the case, usually against a dark background. Not surprisingly, this was a very expensive and time-consuming technique.

The beautiful grande-sonnerie striking carriage clock seen here, with strike selection lever in the base, is decorated in several different shades of gold and with motifs of birds, flowers and foliage. The superbly executed dial – with delicate black Roman numerals laid on white plaques on a pale blue/grey background, with delicate gilt decoration in the centre – is typical of some of Henri Jacot's finer pieces, although the clock is not signed by him. A small alarm disc mimics the decoration on the main dial.

Height: 7¼ in (18.4 cm)

porating such features as a chronometer escapement. Interestingly, when a travelling case was provided this was usually of wood, not leather, as with the French clocks. Whereas in France there were a relatively large number of carriage clock manufacturers, in England production was mostly confined to a few of the top names, such as McCabe, Frodsham, Dent, Vulliamy, Barwise, Smith and Jump.

To try and produce a viable alternative to the French carriage clock, a few small English carriage timepieces with a going barrel (no fusee) and without strike were made, which usually had solid sides and back door. They do not appear to have been a success, however.

Swiss Carriage Clocks
· · · · · ·

The Swiss produced a limited number of carriage clocks similar to those made in the Franche-Comté region of eastern France in the earlier period. Two of the most famous makers were the Courvoisiers, Frédéric and Auguste. One suspects that the majority of the later carriage clocks bearing Swiss names were made either in whole or in part in France. However, from around 1900 to 1930, a most attractive range of miniature Swiss carriage clocks was produced around Geneva by firms such as the Geneva Clock Company. These were usually beautifully decorated with coloured enamels, and the best of them were retailed by firms such as Cartier and Asprey.

Austrian Carriage Clocks
· · · · · ·

The Viennese produced a most attractive series of travelling/carriage clocks between *c*1800 and 1850. These usually had engine-turned, fire-gilt cases, sometimes glazed at the sides and with movements of two-day duration. They frequently incorporated a duplex escapement and struck the quarters on bells or, more commonly, gongs.

American Carriage Clocks
· · · · · ·

A few American firms mass-produced carriage clocks, usually of relatively simple design, sometimes copying those produced in France and in other instances evolving their own distinctive styles.

The Waterbury Clock Company undoubtedly made a large number of carriage clocks, but they were also produced by the Ansonia Clock Company, Chauncey Jerome, Seth Thomas, the Boston Clock Company and the Vermont Clock Company.

Carriage Clock Varieties

To try and give some idea of the vast range of carriage clocks produced, several groups of carriage clocks are shown here. All except the one in the centre top, which is by James McCabe, London, are French.

Some points of interest:

Top Left Beautiful porcelain panels.

Top Right Typical Oriental-style porcelain panels with birds and flowers in a bamboo-style case.

Middle Row Centre A fine early fully engraved French carriage clock with centre-sweep seconds hand, day and date, and with an alarm.

Middle Row Right A fully engraved oval carriage clock, which is always a popular style.

Middle Row, Second from Left A lovely little rococo cased carriage clock. These are comparatively rare.

French Carriage Clocks 1840–1910

TOP ROW

Centre Top A giant *anglaise*-cased grande-sonnerie striking carriage clock with day, date and alarm; *c*1900. Its case is called *anglaise* (English) because the French makers thought its severe, squared-off shape would appeal to English tastes.

CENTRE ROW

Left A Paul Garnier clock, *c*1840.
Centre A carriage clock with a multipiece case, *c*1840, flanked by two lovely little miniatures.
Right A *cornich*-cased clock.

BOTTOM ROW

Left A clock with strike repeat.
Centre A clock with a fine, fully engraved, oval case and with an alarm.
Right An engraved *canelle*-cased carriage clock by Jacot.

— ⑩ —

ENGLISH CARRIAGE CLOCK, S SMITH AND SONS, LONDON, MID 19TH CENTURY

English carriage clocks were only produced in small numbers by a handful of makers such as McCabe, Frodsham, Viner and Smith. They were usually much larger than their French counterparts, although the English did produce a few small carriage clocks that were generally simple timepieces, often without a fusee.

This is a typical English carriage clock in one of the most popular case styles. It has been built virtually to chronometer standards. The chain fusee movement has a jewelled train and a freesprung lever escapement. The white-enamelled dial has a recess for the seconds ring below 12 o'clock and another above 6 o'clock to indicate the state of wind (0 to 8). It is signed by the well-known makers, S Smith and Sons, Trafalgar Square, London, and is surrounded by a gilt mask.

Height: 9⅜ in (23.85 cm)

— ⑪ —

AUSTRIAN CARRIAGE CLOCK,
MICHAEL GRUEBMÜLLNER,
C1800–10

From 1800 to 1850, the Austrians produced some lovely little carriage clocks entirely different from the French models. They were nearly always of only two-day duration, had grande-sonnerie striking, usually with an alarm, and often employed a duplex escapement. Quite often the cases were heavily engraved and fire gilt. Illustrated here is a small early and decorative carriage clock by Michael Gruebmüllner of Waitzen, Austria (present-day Vac, Hungary), with grande-sonnerie strike on two bells and alarm, in a breakarch gilded case with an attractively painted enamel dial showing flowers at the corners and a landscape in the arch. The hinged front door is glazed and there are glazed side panels.

The verge movement with solid brass balance has a chain fusee going train and quarter and hour trains with going barrels. The bells are in the base protected by the decorative skirt.

Height: 6½ in (16.5 cm)

Precision Timekeeping: The Quest for Accuracy on Land and Sea

Our quest for accurate timekeeping has been a dominant theme in life for at least the last millennium and has indeed concerned us for longer than that.

The first major advance came with the invention of the mechanical clock, probably in the late 13th century. The next step forward was the introduction of the pendulum in 1657, closely followed by the introduction of the anchor escapement, coupled with the royal or seconds-beating pendulum some 12 to 14 years later. Over this period clocks had improved in accuracy from an error of maybe 5–10 minutes a day to 15–20 seconds a week.

A further advance was the introduction of maintaining power so that the clock did not stop while it was being wound. The first method devised was known as 'bolt and shutter', which was largely replaced in the 1730s by John Harrison's 'going ratchet'.

Another problem, which became apparent as the accuracy of clocks increased, was the effect of changes in temperature. As it got hotter the pendulum rod would expand and increase in length, thus slowing the clock. To overcome this, two principal forms of compensated pendulum were invented: the mercury-compensated pendulum and the gridiron pendulum. A mercury-compensated pendulum is one that incorporates a glass jar filled with mercury as the bob. As the rod expands down the mercury expands up, thus the effective length of the pendulum remains the same. The gridiron pendulum involves the use of a pendulum rod consisting of rods of iron and brass that are joined in such a way that their expansions cancel each other out.

The problem was finally laid to rest around the year 1900 by the use of a metal known as invar, which has a negligible coefficient of expansion, for the pendulum rod, and keeping precision clocks at constant temperatures with the aid of thermostats and electric heating.

A further refinement was the enclosing of the clock movement within a sealed jar, thus preventing it being affected by any change in barometric pressure.

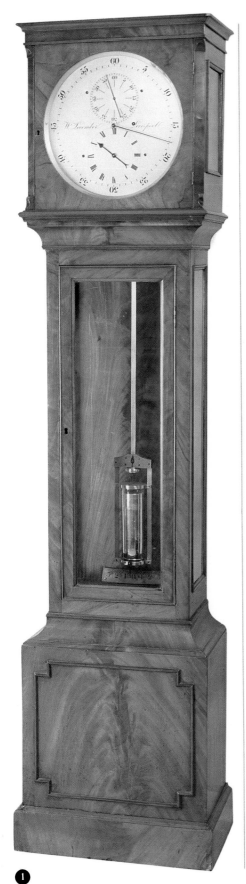

— **①** —

EIGHT-DAY LONGCASE REGULATOR, LECOMBER, LIVERPOOL, C1820

This fine longcase regulator is typical of those produced in the first half of the 19th century. Note the glazed door exposing the mercury-compensated pendulum and the regulator-style silvered-brass dial with a centre-sweep minute hand; a large seconds ring (the most important) is at the top

The superb quality movement has massive plates and pillars to give the clock as much rigidity as possible. The escapement is jewelled to reduce friction and wear to a minimum, the wheels and pinions are excellently executed to increase efficiency and the whole is enclosed in brass dust covers. This typical high-grade regulator would have been capable of keeping time to within as great an accuracy as 1–2 seconds a week.

Height: 6 ft 2 in (1.9 m)

The final problem that had to be overcome on the mechanical clock (prior to its accuracy being vastly exceeded by atomic and other devices) was how to prevent the movement from influencing the isochronicity (regular or even beating) of the pendulum. The ultimate solution, which took some 150 years to arrive at, was achieved by Shortt, who devised a clock with two pendulums, a 'master', which was detached from the movement and thus swung freely, and a 'slave', which had to do the work (ie, it was attached to the movement).

The subject of precision pendulum clocks is a vast and complex one stretching through from Tompion's famous year-duration clocks – which were installed at the Royal Observatory, Greenwich, in the 1670s to decide whether or not the earth rotated at constant speed – right through to the precision machines that were made through the 1940s by famous makers like Reifler, Le Roy and Shortt.

Timekeeping at Sea

By the early 18th century it was realized that good timekeeping at sea was essential for accurate navigation (and also cartography). However, to make a clock that could tolerate the pitching and tossing of a ship was a major undertaking, one which demanded new technology and was beyond the skills of any clockmaker at that time.

To stimulate research the British Admiralty formed a Board of Longitude empowered to award a prize of up to £20,000, an enormous sum in those days, to anyone who could devise a method of determining longitude at sea, which in practice meant devising an accurate sea clock.

2

— **2** —

TWO-DAY CHRONOMETER, BROCKBANK & ATKINS NO 1159, LONDON, C1870

Seen here is a two-day chronometer suspended on gimbals in a brass-bound, three-tier mahogany box. The dial has the standard chronometer layout with gold centre-sweep minute and hour hands, a very delicate blued-steel seconds hand in the bottom part of the dial and the state of wind indication (up/down graduated in hours) below 12 o'clock. A locking device for the gimbals may be seen at the front right, and the winding key, which can only be turned in one direction, is at the back on the same side. Carrying handles are provided. The release button for the top lid is situated just below this lid.

This chronometer is a typical example of the hundreds of thousands of chronometers produced from *c*1820 to 1950, mostly in England, for use by the navies of the world.

— **3** —

TWO-DAY CHRONOMETER PARKINSON & FRODSHAM, CHANGE ALLEY, LONDON NO 3234, C1850

A mid-19th-century two-day marine chronometer suspended in gimbals and contained in a three-tier brass-bound mahogany box.

It was the dedication, determination and genius of one man, John Harrison (1693–1776), assisted in the early days by his brother, James, who, finally, over a period of some 40 years, overcame this problem. He received the final part of his reward when he was nearly 80. It was left to other men such as John Arnold and Thomas Earnshaw to make Harrison's invention a practical proposition, simplifying its production so that it could be made in quantity without losing any of its accuracy. The term now applied to these sea clocks is chronometers. They are contained in three-tier wooden boxes and supported by brass gimbals, so that whatever the movement of the ship the chronometer remains horizontal. To read the time only the top lid needs to be lifted, leaving the chronometer still protected by the lower lid, which has a glazed top.

Index

Picture Credits

Numbers refer to pages. T = *Top;* B = *Bottom;* L = *Left;* R = *Right.*